THE PREHISTORIC EARTH

DAWN OF THE DINOSAUR AGE

THE LATE TRIASSIC & EARLY JURASSIC EPOCHS

THE PREHISTORIC EARTH

THE PREHISTORIC EARTH

DAWN OF THE DINOSAUR AGE

THE LATE TRIASSIC & EARLY JURASSIC EPOCHS

Thom Holmes

CHELSEA HOUSE
PUBLISHERS
An imprint of Infobase Publishing

THE PREHISTORIC EARTH: Dawn of the Dinosaur Age

Copyright © 2008 by Infobase Publishing

Chelsea House
An imprint of Infobase Publishing
132 West 31st Street
New York NY 10001

Library of Congress Cataloging-in-Publication Data

Holmes, Thom.
  Dawn of the dinosaur age / Thom Holmes.
    p. cm. — (The prehistoric Earth)
  Includes bibliographical references and index.
  ISBN 978-0-8160-5960-7 (hardcover)
  1. Dinosaurs—Study and teaching—United States. 2. Fossils—Study and teaching—United States.
3. Geology, Stratigraphic—Mesozoic. I. Title. II. Series.

  QE861.4.H65 2008
  567.9—dc22   2007045331

Text design by Kerry Casey
Cover design by Salvatore Luongo
Section opener images © John Sibbick

Printed in the United States of America

Bang NMSG 10 9 8 7 6 5 4 3 2 1

This book is printed on acid-free paper.

All links and Web addresses were checked and verified to be correct at the time of publication. Because of the dynamic nature of the Web, some addresses and links may have changed since publication and may no longer be valid.

CONTENTS

PREFACE

To be curious about the future, one must know something about the past.

Humans have been recording events in the world around them for about 5,300 years. That is how long it has been since the Sumerian people, in a land that today is southern Iraq, invented the first known written language. Writing allowed people to document what they saw happening around them. The written word gave a new permanency to life. Language, and writing in particular, made history possible.

History is a marvelous human invention, but how do people know about things that happened before language existed? Or before humans existed? Events that took place before human record keeping began are called *prehistory*. Prehistoric life is, by its definition, any life that existed before human beings existed and were able to record for posterity what was happening in the world around them.

Prehistory is as much a product of the human mind as history. Scientists who specialize in unraveling clues of prehistoric life are called *paleontologists*. They study life that existed before human history, often hundreds of thousands and millions of years in the past. Their primary clues come from fossils of animals and plants and from geologic evidence about Earth's topography and climate. Through the skilled and often imaginative interpretation of fossils, paleontologists are able to reconstruct the appearance, lifestyle, environment, and relationships of ancient life-forms. While paleontology is grounded in a study of prehistoric life, it draws on many other sciences to complete an accurate picture of the past. Information from the fields of biology, zoology, geology, chemistry, meteorology, and even astrophysics is called into play to help the paleontologist view the past through the lens of today's knowledge.

If a writer were to write a history of all sports, would it be enough to write only about table tennis? Certainly not. On the shelves of bookstores and libraries, however, we find just such a slanted perspective toward the story of the dinosaurs. Dinosaurs have captured our imagination at the expense of many other equally fascinating, terrifying, and unusual creatures. Dinosaurs were not alone in the pantheon of prehistoric life, but it is rare to find a book that also mentions the many other kinds of life that came before and after the dinosaurs.

The Prehistoric Earth is a series that explores the evolution of life from its earliest forms 3.5 billion years ago until the emergence of modern humans some 300,000 years ago. Four volumes in the series trace the story of the dinosaurs. Six other volumes are devoted to the kinds of animals that evolved before, during, and after the reign of the dinosaurs. *The Prehistoric Earth* covers the early explosion of life in the oceans; the invasion of the land by the first land animals; the rise of fishes, amphibians, reptiles, mammals, and birds; and the emergence of modern humans.

The Prehistoric Earth series is written for readers in high school. Based on the latest scientific findings in paleontology, *The Prehistoric Earth* is the most comprehensive and up-to-date series of its kind for this age group.

The first volume in the series, *Early Life*, offers foundational information about geologic time, Earth science, fossils, the classification of organisms, and evolution. This volume also begins the chronological exploration of fossil life that explodes with the incredible life-forms of Precambrian times and the Cambrian Period, more than 500 million years ago.

The remaining nine volumes in the series can be read chronologically. Each volume covers a specific geologic time period and describes the major forms of life that lived at that time. The books also trace the geologic forces and climate changes that affected the evolution of life through the ages. Readers of *The Prehistoric Earth* will see the whole picture of prehistoric life take shape. They will learn about forces that affect life on Earth, the directions that life can sometimes take, and ways in which all life-forms depend on each other in the environment. Along the way, readers also will meet many of the scientists who have made remarkable discoveries about the prehistoric Earth.

The language of science is used throughout this series, with ample definition and with an extensive glossary provided in each volume. Important concepts involving geology, evolution, and the lifestyles of early animals are presented logically, step by step. Illustrations, photographs, tables, and maps reinforce and enhance the books' presentation of the story of prehistoric life.

While telling the story of prehistoric life, the author hopes that many readers will be sufficiently intrigued to continue studies on their own. For this purpose, throughout each volume, special "Think About It" sidebars offer additional insights or interesting exercises for readers who wish to explore certain topics. Each book in the series also provides a chapter-by-chapter bibliography of books, journals, and Web sites.

Only about one-tenth of 1 percent of all species of prehistoric animals are known from fossils. A multitude of discoveries remain to be made in the field of paleontology. It is with earnest, best wishes that I hope that some of these discoveries will be made by readers inspired by this series.

—Thom Holmes
Jersey City, New Jersey

ACKNOWLEDGMENTS

I would like to thank the many dedicated and hardworking people at Chelsea House. A special debt of gratitude goes to my editors, Shirley White, Brian Belval, and Frank Darmstadt, for their support and guidance in conceiving and making *The Prehistoric Earth* a reality. Frank and Brian were instrumental in fine-tuning the features of the series as well as accepting my ambitious plan for creating a comprehensive reference for students. Brian greatly influenced the development of the color-illustration program and supported my efforts to integrate the work of some of the best artists in the field, most notably John Sibbick, whose work appears throughout the set. Shirley's excellent questions about the science behind the books contributed greatly to the readability of the result. The excellent copyediting of Mary Ellen Kelly was both thoughtful and vital to shaping the final manuscript. I thank Mary Ellen for her patience as well as her valuable review and suggestions that help make the books a success.

I am privileged to have worked with some of the brightest minds in paleontology on this series. Jerry D. Harris, the director of paleontology at Dixie State College in St. George, Utah, reviewed the draft of *Dawn of the Dinosaur Age* and made many important suggestions that affected the course of the work. Jerry also wrote the Foreword for the volume.

In many ways, a set of books such as this requires years of preparation. Some of the work is educational, and I owe much gratitude to Dr. Peter Dodson of the University of Pennsylvania for his gracious and inspiring tutelage over the years. Another dimension of preparation requires experience digging fossils, and for giving me these opportunities I thank my friends and colleagues who have taken me into the field with them, including Phil Currie, Rodolfo Coria,

Matthew Lammana, and Ruben Martinez. Finally comes the work needed to put thoughts down on paper and complete the draft of a book, a process that always takes many more hours than I plan on. I thank Anne for bearing with my constant state of busy-ness and for helping me remember the important things in life. You are an inspiration to me. I also thank my daughter, Shaina, the genius in the family and another inspiration, for always being supportive and humoring her father's obsession with prehistoric life.

FOREWORD

Life is change. As clichéd—and, perhaps, oversimplistic—as this sounds, it is still a fact; and nowhere is this fact better expressed than in the fossil record, the only record we have of how and when life underwent change in the deep past. Paleontologists are scientists dedicated to documenting and deciphering the fossil record to see how and why life has changed through time. By doing so, they establish our understanding of how life responds to environmental changes and our knowledge of what limits that change—issues that are critical to humans today as we begin to see significant changes in our modern world's climate.

Thus, to try to understand the history of life on Earth is not simply a pointless pastime; it is an important scientific pursuit. Our understanding of life's past diversity has become so good, however, that it is easy to get lost in the abundance of information available. This series, *The Prehistoric Earth*, is a terrific place to begin for anyone with curiosity about the history of life on Earth, even if that person never becomes a degreed scientist. Regardless of what kinds of fossil organisms interest someone, this series has something for that person and will help him or her to understand what the ancient world was like at different points in time.

Paleontology is an interesting science. It is actually a combination of many sciences, predominantly Earth science (geology) and life science (biology), but it also requires a good amount of chemistry, physics, and even astronomy. This may be why paleontologists are hard to place in universities—at some, they are in geology departments; in others, they are in biology departments. Fortunately, Thom Holmes melds these seemingly disparate sciences together in *The Prehistoric Earth*. He provides excellent summaries that will open doors for further investigation by all interested readers.

If this is the first book in the series that you are reading, I heartily recommend that you read the others, too; they will help you to put everything in the best possible context.

The book you now are reading, *Dawn of the Dinosaur Age*, explores one of the most important times in Earth history: the beginning of the Mesozoic Era. The book emphasizes the recovery of life, during the Triassic Period, from the massive extinction event—the largest in Earth's history—that brought the Paleozoic Era to a close. As life expanded into the myriad ecological niches emptied by the extinction event, it produced, by the end of the Triassic, all the major "players" that still dominate the world today: the first turtles, crocodylomorphs, mammals, and—perhaps most evocatively and famously—dinosaurs. How dinosaurs evolved is a fascinating story. It is not often told outside the technical, scientific literature and is rarely as up to date as Thom Holmes has told it here. So sit back and enjoy. You are about to learn about a wide variety of spectacular and bizarre organisms. Many of them you probably never have heard of before, but you will not soon forget them.

—Dr. Jerry D. Harris
Director of Paleontology
Dixie State College
St. George, Utah

INTRODUCTION

The **evolution** and diversification of the first organisms on Earth progressed even in the face of tumultuous changes to the planet and devastating events leading to several **mass extinctions**. Life in the Paleozoic **Era** was marked by large-scale changes to geology and **climate**. Those who study the history of life view the end of the Paleozoic as a kind of curtain being drawn on evolution's first great span of "experiments." Striking Earth's stage with a bang, the mass extinction at the end of the Paleozoic almost left that stage utterly empty of life. Life in every region of the globe—in the sea, in lakes and streams, and on land—nearly perished entirely. The end of the Paleozoic also marked the beginning of a new span in the history of life, the evolution of modern **flora** and **fauna** with often-distant but direct links to organisms alive today.

Vertebrates in the sea and on the land emerged from the devastating effects of the end-Permian mass extinction diminished but on the rebound. *Dawn of the Dinosaur Age* presents the first act in the drama that would become the Mesozoic Era, the sorting out of various terrestrial (land-based) fauna, and the introduction of the first dinosaurs as the leading actors of the new world.

OVERVIEW OF *DAWN OF THE DINOSAUR AGE*

Dawn of the Dinosaur Age begins, in Section One, by looking at the geological and climatic aftermath of the end-Permian **extinction** and the conditions of the early Mesozoic Era that created opportunities for archosaurian vertebrates, including dinosaurs. Chapter 1 describes the widespread changes to ocean and land environments, including worldwide changes to climates that served as catalysts for the spread of the archosaurs. Among these changes was another important set of mass-extinction events at the end of the Triassic

Period. Chapter 2 introduces the archosaurs of the Early Triassic that led to the rise of the dinosaurs and their relatives. In Chapter 3, the earliest dinosaurs are described, along with reasons for their rapid rise to a position of dominance over many other animals of the Mesozoic Era. Was their success due to good luck, or to better **genes**?

Section Two, *Dinosaurs of the Early Mesozoic Era,* introduces the major groups of dinosaurs. Chapter 4 presents the two major divisions of dinosaurs: the **Saurischia**, or "lizard-hipped" dinosaurs, and the **Ornithischia**, or "bird-hipped" dinosaurs. The chapter then goes on to look closely at the **carnivorous** saurischian dinosaurs: their traits, their lifestyles, and the earliest examples of their kind. Chapter 5 describes the early evolution of the other major **clade** of saurischians, the giant, long-necked **herbivores**. The chapter explores their early evolution, their traits, and the **adaptations** that led to their great success. Chapter 6 describes the origin and traits of the earliest members of the Ornithischia, the other major dinosaur clade, which consisted of diverse plant eaters.

Each chapter uses tables, maps, figures, and photos to depict the life, habitat, and changing evolutionary patterns that affected the lives of the early dinosaurs and their kin. Several chapters also include "Think About It" sidebars that elaborate on interesting issues, people, and discoveries related to Mesozoic life.

Dawn of the Dinosaur Age builds on foundational principles of geology, **fossils**, and the study of life. Readers who want to refresh their knowledge of certain basic terms and principles in the study of past life—or who seek to learn those principles for the first time—may wish to consult the glossary in the back of *Dawn of the Dinosaur Age.* Perhaps most important to keep in mind are the basic rules governing evolution: The direction of evolution is set in motion first by the genetically determined traits inherited by individuals, coupled with the interaction of that individual with its habitat. Changes accumulate, generation after generation, and allow **species** to adapt to changing conditions in the world around them. As Charles Darwin (1809–1882) explained, "The small differences distinguishing varieties of the same species steadily tend to increase, till they equal the greater differences between species of the same **genus**, or even of distinct genera." These are the rules of nature that drove the engine of evolution during the Paleozoic and gave rise to forms of life whose descendants still populate the Earth.

SECTION ONE:
THE WORLD
OF THE DINOSAURS

THE MESOZOIC WORLD

The end-Permian mass extinction marked a significant milestone in the history of life. It signaled a passing from the Paleozoic Era, the time of ancient organisms, to the Mesozoic Era, the time of "middle life." Placed squarely at the helm of planet Earth were the reptiles, whose ascendancy was already assured as the Permian Period came to a close. Not all lines of Paleozoic reptiles survived to cross the timeline into the Mesozoic, but their numbers and diversity were such that several key groups lived to propagate distinctive groups of reptiles that would dominate life in every major habitat.

The Mesozoic Era is divided into three **periods** of time. It begins with the Triassic, moves to the middle or Jurassic Period, and concludes with the Cretaceous Period. These periods are further divided into smaller spans, all of which are shown, along with major milestones, in the table below that outlines the evolution of Mesozoic vertebrates. Mass extinctions are also noted in the following table to illustrate how new species evolve to occupy niches left vacant by extinct species. The Mesozoic Era spanned 180 million years, and dinosaurs ruled over terrestrial life for nearly 160 million of those years.

During the Mesozoic Era, gradual changes in Earth's tectonic plates modified land and ocean habitats. This affected the world's many life-forms. This chapter examines the geologic and climatic conditions that influenced the evolution of the flora and fauna of the days of the dinosaurs.

EVOLUTIONARY MILESTONES OF THE MESOZOIC ERA

Period	Epoch	Span (millions of years ago)	Duration (millions of years)	Organismal Milestones
Triassic	Early Triassic	251–245	6	Diversification and distribution of amniotes, particularly synapsid and diapsid reptiles
	Middle Triassic	245–228	17	Rise of pterosaurs and euryapsid marine reptiles
	Late Triassic	228–200	28	Early dinosaurs and mammals
	Mass extinction			Casualties: dicynodonts, carnivorous cynodonts, phytosaurs, placodonts, nothosaurs
Jurassic	Early Jurassic	200–175	25	Radiation of carnivorous and herbivorous dinosaurs; first crocodiles
	Middle Jurassic	175–161	14	Rise of armored and plated dinosaurs; rise of sauropods
	Late Jurassic	161–145	16	Diversification of sauropods; the theropods; the first birds
Cretaceous	Early Cretaceous	145–100	45	Continued diversification of dinosaurs, marine reptiles, and pterosaurs
	Late Cretaceous	100–65.5	35	Rise of large theropods, horned dinosaurs, hadrosaurs
	Mass extinction			Casualties: dinosaurs, marine reptiles, pterosaurs

RESHAPING OF THE CONTINENTS AND OCEANS

The Earth underwent dramatic geologic changes during the 180 million-year span of the Mesozoic Era. During most of the Triassic Period, the continents that are known today were still joined together as the supercontinent **Pangaea**. Pangaea was an expansive landmass that filled most of the Earth's Western Hemisphere. Because of Pangaea's size, distinct interior climate zones and new habitats for plants and animals developed. The formation of Pangaea also marked a low ebb in ocean depths; this was one of the factors that contributed to the changes in ocean habitats that led to the end-Permian extinction of many marine invertebrate species.

By the Early Jurassic, Pangaea began to split apart, first dividing into two landmasses. The northern landmass, which geologists call Laurasia, included areas that later became North America, Europe, and Asia. The southern landmass, known as Gondwana, included the regions now known as South America, Africa, India, Australia, and Antarctica. Further division into the present configuration of the world's continents was well under way by the end of the Mesozoic Era.

If the formation of Pangaea could be called the signature geologic event of the Paleozoic, then the gradual breakup of the supercontinent could be called the most influential geologic occurrence of the Mesozoic. Massive shifts in tectonic plates were not without their consequences for many of the world's habitats. While Pangaea was intact, it was surrounded by the **Panthalassic Ocean**, the southeastern portion of which was called the **Tethys Ocean**. The Atlantic Ocean began to appear in the middle of Pangaea as tectonic plates separated and continental landmasses radiated outward from the equator to the north and south. The collision of tectonic plates began the formation of North America. Continental areas today associated with North and South America, Europe, central Asia, and northern Africa were the site of extensive inland seas. By the Cretaceous Period, North America had a shallow inland sea stretching down its middle from what is now Alaska to the Gulf of Mexico.

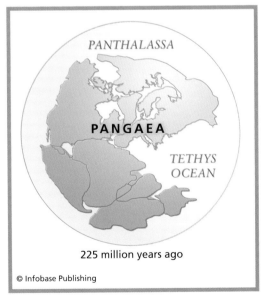

225 million years ago

© Infobase Publishing

Pangaea during the Triassic Period

CLIMATES AND HABITATS

The world of the Mesozoic was evenly temperate in climate over most of the globe. Unlike the second half of the Paleozoic, during which the most habitable landmasses consisted of tropical rain forests on either side of the equator, the spreading of the continents northward and southward during the Mesozoic was accompanied by climate changes. These changes led to a moderately warm but drier environment during most of the Mesozoic. One reason for this moderating of global temperature was the breakup of Pangaea itself. The division of the giant landmass into smaller continents made all land more susceptible to temperature changes moderated by ocean currents. During the Mesozoic, Earth was covered by more water than had covered it during the latter stages of the Paleozoic, and there were no massive ice caps at the poles. Because water is a tremendous sponge for solar radiation, the oceans became warm, and ocean currents distributed heat to the north and to the south. This distribution provided a more evenly temperate world climate than had existed in the previous era.

Fossil evidence of nontropical plants distributed all over the globe and the lack of any evidence for glaciation support the likelihood that the climate of the Mesozoic was pleasantly mild. Lands that are now known to be extremely cold to the north—such as Greenland and northern Europe—once hosted such mild-climate plants as ginkgo and conifer trees. None of these plants could have survived subfreezing temperatures on a regular basis.

Analysis of the oxygen-isotope content—a direct indicator of climate—of Mesozoic marine fossils provides additional support for a temperate world climate. Samples taken from locations in North America, Europe, and Russia show that the temperature of shallow marine environments ranged from 60°F to 75°F (15°C to 24°C), making for a relatively warm day at the Mesozoic beach most of the time.

By the Late Mesozoic, the world's dry, temperate climate had become more humid in some locations, such as ancient North America. This was partly due to the fact that a warm, shallow sea ran down the middle of the continent. This inland sea provided continually large volumes of evaporation and periodic downpours of rain to support a robust recycling of atmospheric moisture.

MASS EXTINCTIONS OF THE LATE TRIASSIC EPOCH

The end-Permian mass extinction nearly wiped out all life on the planet. Those animals that stumbled into the Triassic Period and the era of "middle life" required 10 million years to return to previous levels of diversity. Marine animals and coral reefs took even longer to recover. Many families of plants survived the end-Permian extinction in relatively good numbers, but gradual changes in climate and habitats saw the once-dominant broadleaf seed ferns and cordaites replaced by conifers, cycads, ginkgoes, and spore-bearing plants such as club mosses, ferns, and horsetails. The dominant land animals of the Early to Middle Triassic were the rhynchosaurs, dicynodonts, and cynodonts, many of which had successfully migrated to the farthest corners of Pangaea prior to its gradual breakup into small landmasses.

The newfound stability of the Early to Middle Triassic did not last. Between 228 million and 199.6 million years ago, in the Late Triassic Epoch, two more mass-extinction events laid waste large numbers of animals and plants. Among those devastated were the fiercest **predators** and largest herbivores of the time, including the rhynchosaurs, most dicynodonts and cynodonts, and even some archosaurs. Plants also suffered greatly: The newly dominant seed ferns—including conifers, cycads, and ginkgoes—and the spore-bearing club mosses were nearly wiped out and supplanted by other conifers, larger cycads, and surviving mosses. These extinctions have been blamed on climate shifts, the first of which may have been caused by a likely asteroid impact, as evidenced by the 43-mile (70 km) diameter Manicouagan Crater in Quebec, Canada.

Curiously, the Late Triassic extinctions coincided with the appearance of the first dinosaurs—an association that is the subject of much scientific debate that will be explored in Chapter 3. Chapter 2 explores the rise of the archosaurs, or "ruling reptiles," and the likely reasons for their early success.

Late Traissic landscape

SUMMARY

This chapter examined the geologic and climatic conditions that influenced the evolution of the flora and fauna of the days of the dinosaurs.

1. The end-Permian mass extinction marked the passage from the Paleozoic Era of "ancient life" to the beginning of the Mesozoic Era of "middle life."
2. The Mesozoic Era is divided into three major time spans: the Triassic Period, the Jurassic Period, and the Cretaceous Period.

3. Dinosaurs and their reptile kin in the oceans and in the air were the dominant vertebrates of the Mesozoic Era.

4. Geologically, the Mesozoic Era is noted for the gradual breakup of the supercontinent Pangaea into the landmasses that would become today's continents.

5. The climate of the Mesozoic Era was evenly temperate over most of the globe.

6. Two mass extinctions during the Late Triassic Epoch wiped out many ancient lines of reptiles and gave way to the rise of the first dinosaurs.

ARCHOSAURS: THE RULING REPTILES

By the start of the Middle Triassic Epoch, 245 million years ago, three evolutionary lines of amniotes had become well established. The fundamental anatomical trait used by **paleontologists** to differentiate these groups is the absence or presence of different numbers of **temporal fenestrae**—the small holes, or "windows"—in the temple region on the sides and top of the skull. These openings in the skull provided a spot for complex groups of jaw muscles to attach and made the skull lighter. The presence of these temporal fenestrae contributed to the adaptability of some amniotes to varied food sources and improved their innate swiftness without sacrificing bone strength. The result was a blossoming of amniote types and adaptations that ranged from bulky herbivores such as *Lystrosaurus* (South Africa, India, China, Russia, and Antarctica), with jaws adapted for more efficient chewing of plants, to lightweight but deadly predators such as *Euparkeria* (South Africa).

The roots of all of today's terrestrial amniotes—vertebrates that protect the embryos of their offspring within the sealed environment of an amniotic egg—are found in three lines of reptiles that originated in the Late Paleozoic and diversified in the Mesozoic Era.

Anapsida. These are amniotes with no temporal fenestrae, including the earliest reptiles. This group includes the early reptiles *Hylonomus* and *Paleothyris* and several other extinct Late Carboniferous-to-Triassic reptiles such as pareiasaurs and procolophonids. The group also includes living tortoises and turtles.

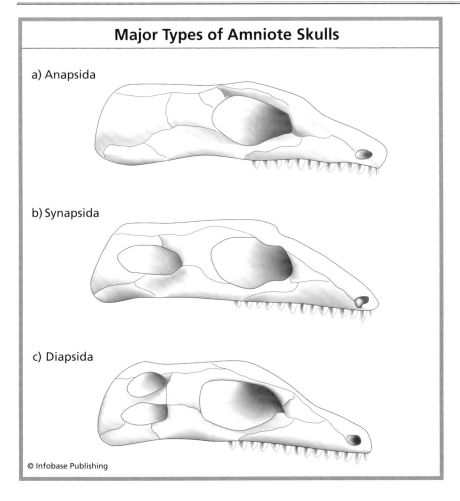

Major Types of Amniote Skulls

a) Anapsida

b) Synapsida

c) Diapsida

© Infobase Publishing

Synapsida. These are amniotes (but not reptiles) with one temporal fenestra on each side of the skull, positioned somewhat behind and below the orbit, or eye opening. This group includes all mammals as well as extinct "mammal-like reptiles." Synapsids first appeared in the middle of the Carboniferous Period.

Diapsida. These are amniotes with two temporal fenestrae on each side: a lower one like the one seen in synapsids, and another one just above it, on top of the skull and behind the orbit. Lizards, snakes, crocodylians, and birds are included in this group, as are extinct dinosaurs and pterosaurs (flying reptiles). Diapsids first appeared in the Late Carboniferous Period. The diapsids also include extinct marine reptiles such as nothosaurs, plesiosaurs, and ichthyosaurs, most of which thrived in the Mesozoic Era. Marine reptiles secondarily, and independently of other diapsids, lost one of their temporal fenestrae.

Of these four groups, the Diapsida became the most prevalent amniote group of the Mesozoic. The biggest reptilian success story of all time encompassed the rule of the dinosaurs and their kin. The remainder of this chapter examines the roots, diversification, and relationships of the early archosaurs that led to the rise of the dinosaurs.

THE ARCHOSAURIAN DIAPSIDS

The diapsids are divided into two primary groups, the Lepidosauromorpha and the Archosauromorpha. The **Lepidosauria**, a subgroup of the Lepidosauromorphs, includes lizards and snakes and their extinct ancestors. During the Mesozoic, this group of highly diverse but small animals lived in the shadows of the dinosaurs.

The **Archosauria**, or "ruling reptiles," was a subgroup of the Archosauromorpha and represented a commanding lineage of amniotes that includes pterosaurs, dinosaurs, crocodylians, and birds. The archosaurs were distinguished from other diapsids by a number of anatomical features. These included an additional opening in the side of the skull called an **antorbital fenestra** that was positioned just in front of the eye orbit. Early archosaurs of the Triassic Period that were not dinosaurs, crocodylians, or pterosaurs make up a **paraphyletic** group referred to as **basal** archosaurs. It is from the basal archosaurs that all later archosaurian reptiles arose.

There was another group of archosauromorphs that were not archosaurians ("archosaurs" in the usual sense), including protorosaurs, erythrosuchids, rhynchosaurs, and *Euparkeria*. These are sometimes referred to as "proto-archosaurs" because they share some but not all of the traits that are found in archosaurs and they are considered evolutionarily more basal.

By the Middle Triassic, the diversification of most archosaurs was following two divergent paths. One lineage, the Crurotarsi ("cross ankles"), eventually led to the evolution of crocodylians. The other lineage led to pterosaurs, dinosaurs, and eventually birds, collectively known as the Ornithodira ("bird necks"). The anatomical differences between the crurotarsans and the ornithodirans are most evident in their limb structure and posture. While several other kinds of archosaurs were common by the end of the Triassic Period, only representatives of the crurotarsans and the ornithodirans survived the end-Triassic extinctions and moved on to flourish, in one form or another, ever since.

Crocodylians and other **extant** reptiles have a *sprawling* posture. This means that their limbs extend outward to the sides, and their bodies are lifted just a little off the ground, as needed, when the animals walk or run. When resting, a sprawling animal will lie on its belly to take the weight off of its limbs. In this resting position, the limbs of a sprawling animal cannot be tucked beneath the body. Instead, the limbs must flex at the knee or elbow joint so that the legs can point comfortably upward and still be capable of lifting the body up at a moment's notice in case the animal needs to move. The sprawling animal has strong, well-developed muscle groups along the underside of the body and tail to enable it to rise up and lower down and walk with its limbs swinging out from the sides. The muscles and strength needed to accomplish this feat are considerable. A human lying on his or her stomach with outstretched arms and legs will find it nearly impossible to lift the body off the ground by pushing up from the knees and elbows. Humans, not having a sprawling posture, do not have the specialized muscle groups to make this weight-lifting exercise a success.

A sprawling posture makes it difficult for an animal to sustain extended periods of running, however. Crocodylians are powerful animals in many respects, but they cannot run for more than a short burst because of the energy requirements of holding up body weight with a sprawling posture. One constraint of their sprawling posture is that the lungs are compressed by the locomotive bending of the body. Modern crurotarsans have a sprawling posture, and it is also seen in other reptiles and amphibians, but many of the early crurotarsans had an upright gait suited for walking on land.

Dinosaurs and other ornithodirans had a fully *erect* posture, in which the limbs (two or four) were positioned underneath the body. While associated with archosaurs such as dinosaurs, an erect posture also evolved independently in the cynodonts and their kin, the mammals. An erect posture is also seen in the only surviving descendants of the dinosaurs, the birds. An erect posture offers several advantages. Legs tucked underneath the body can more easily support the weight of the body while also lengthening the stride. These advantages not only make animals with erect postures potentially faster and more agile, they also allow for increased body size, a trait that some dinosaurs took to extremes that have never again been equaled in the history of land animals.

The development of an erect posture in archosaurs led to several changes in the skeletal **anatomy** of the shoulder girdle, the hips, and the ankles. Shoulder and hips were modified so that the attachment of leg bones provided for a more upright stance, with the limbs fully absorbing the weight of the body. The ankles and wrists also became modified in such a way that they provided a stronger, more flexible hinge for the twisting and bending of the feet and hands; this enabled quicker and more sure-footed walking and running.

Basal Archosaurs: Before the Dinosaurs

Basal archosaurs were the stock from which all later archosaurs arose. These early archosaurs were once known by the scientific term Thecodontia, a name given to them by British paleontologist Richard Owen (1804–1892) in 1859. This group originally included any and all archosaurs that dated from the Triassic Period but were not clearly dinosaurs or crocodiles. Although it was assumed that "thecodonts" had a common **tetrapod** ancestor, the evolutionary relationships among the descendants of this ancestor, called **Tetrapoda**, were not clear. Although "thecodonts" shared a few rudimentary traits that united all archosaurs, paleontologists found many differences in "thecodonts" that prevented their being joined into neatly defined groups. This made "thecodonts" a paraphyletic assemblage—an unnatural **taxon** of organisms that did not include all of the descendants of their common ancestor.

In the more than 148 years since Owen named the Thecodontia, paleontology has been kind to its practitioners when it comes to the discovery of Triassic reptiles. Much more is known now than in 1859 about the kinds and varieties of archosaurs that led up to the appearance of dinosaurs, pterosaurs, and crocodylians. While some significant information gaps remain, particularly with regard to painting a complete picture of the earliest of the archosaurs, scientific knowledge about the rise and diversification of archosaurs has made possible a more robust assessment of which archosaurs were related to each other in the Triassic Period. Because they now have more abundant data about these fossils, paleontologists have been able to use **cladistic analysis** to rethink the classification of archosaurs.

Cladistic analysis, or cladistics, is an analytical technique for comparing the **morphological** features, DNA sequences, and behavior of taxa. The primary focus of this analysis is the features of the organisms' skeletons. Organisms are said to be members of the same clade if they are all the descendants of a single common ancestor, even if the common ancestor is yet unknown.

Using cladistics, organisms are classified by their shared characteristics. These shared characteristics confirm the evolutionary links that bind different species into related groups and may also reveal subtle aspects of the skeleton, such as a slight bony ridge on a hip bone or the shape of a joint that connects two limb bones. Given enough well-preserved fossil specimens of specific animals, paleontologists can analyze morphological features statistically to unite species that share the most traits.

In the past 20 years, much work has been done in cladistics to improve the understanding of the evolutionary connections among early archosaur groups. One landmark study was that of paleontologist Jacques A. Gauthier (b. 1951), now of Yale University. In 1986,

Gauthier published a paper in which he used cladistic analysis to explain the origin of birds from theropod dinosaurs. In the course of his analysis, Gauthier also suggested that some of the archosaurs that once were placed within the category of "thecodonts" be united into a group of related animals that he called Ornithodira: the dinosaurs, pterosaurs, birds, and proto-dinosaurs discussed below. Gauthier's important research jump-started an effort that continues to this day to apply cladistic analysis to an understanding of dinosaur evolution.

Several years after Gauthier's landmark work, a paleontologist named Paul Sereno (b. 1957), from the University of Chicago, applied similar cladistic techniques to clarify the origin of crurotarsan archosaurs and early dinosaurs. Sereno is one of today's best-known fossil explorers and has made field discoveries on five continents. Much of his early work involved the exploration of Triassic fossil beds in South America. This gave him an opportunity to study and unearth new specimens of archosaurs that spanned the time associated with the origin of dinosaurs. In 1991, Sereno published a study that united several taxa of archosaurs into the Crurotarsi, the crocodylians and their relatives.

Gauthier and Sereno could not fit all of the known archosaurs into the ornithodirans and crurotarsans. This left a veritable waste bin of remaining taxa that were difficult to classify. Richard Owen's term *Thecodontia* was abandoned in favor of simply calling the remaining known animals basal, or early, archosaurs.

Basal archosaurs include several intriguing kinds of reptiles that thrived from the Late Permian to the end of the Triassic. Many were generally lizardlike in appearance, yet unrelated to the lineage of true lizards, which belong to the other branch of the Diapsida, the Lepidosauromorpha. These early archosaurs had the antorbital fenestra found in the skulls of all later archosaurs. Basal archosaurs also had teeth that were embedded in sockets in the jaw, a trait that would be passed along to dinosaurs and other archosaurs. The waste bin of basal archosaurs also contains several distinctive groups of reptiles whose family lines were well established before some members of the

Archosauria split into the major surviving lineages of the Crurotarsi and Ornithodira.

The Proto-Archosaurs

The end-Permian extinction wiped out many of the terrestrial plants and animals that dominated the end of the Paleozoic Era. As the Triassic got under way, the drier, more temperate climate brought about turnover in both flora and fauna. Spore-bearing tropical plants gave way to seed ferns and conifers. This change may have devastated many lines of amniote herbivores that did not adapt rapidly enough to the changing food supply. Along with those plant-eaters went many of the large-bodied carnivores, thus clearing the way for a new cast of players in the Early Triassic.

Among the plant eaters that survived the end-Permian extinction was *Lystrosaurus*, a bulky beast that can be likened to a "pig-reptile." This plodding synapsid measured about 3.3 feet (1 m) long. It used a pair of tusklike teeth and a beaklike jaw to snip away the tough-bodied vegetation that earlier herbivores probably could not eat easily. Because fossil remains of *Lystrosaurus* are found in such widespread locations as China, Russia, India, South Africa, and Antarctica, they provide evidence that these continents were once connected, at the beginning of the Mesozoic Era. *Lystrosaurus* was a dicynodont, not an archosaur, but it may have been one of the creatures hunted as prey by the first carnivorous members of the ruling reptiles.

One early carnivorous archosaur was *Proterosuchus* (South Africa). It measured about 5 feet (1.5 m) long, including its long tail, and had a skull that was vaguely lizardlike, a crocodile-like body with sprawling posture, and a long neck unlike that seen in either lizards or crocodylians. With its relatively short legs, *Proterosuchus* was probably not a fast runner. It has been found in South African fossil habitats that once were part of a wet floodplain. This suggests that *Proterosuchus* may have lived a life similar to that of modern crocodylians, dwelling near the shore and scrambling through shallow waters to catch trapped fish and slow-moving amphibians.

A close relative of *Proterosuchus* was *Erythrosuchus*, a much larger predator that was better adapted for hunting on land and that also was found in Early Triassic deposits of South Africa. *Erythrosuchus* and its Russian relative *Vjushkovia* developed changes to hips, limbs, and digits that improved these animals' speed and agility on land. Each of these archosaurian predators was the largest carnivore in its habitat; both approached the enormous bulk that medium-sized dinosaurs would enjoy later in the Mesozoic. *Erythrosuchus* measured about 6.6 feet (2 m) long, and *Vjushkovia* measured an astounding 17 feet (5 m). Their skulls were long and narrow, and their jaws were filled with sharp, conical teeth for grasping and tearing prey. They probably made quick business of relatively defenseless dicynodonts such as *Lystrosaurus*.

Another enigmatic basal archosaur from the Early Triassic was *Euparkeria*, a two-foot (60 cm) creature found in Early Triassic rocks of South Africa. With long and powerful hind legs, a strong neck, and a mouth full of recurved, biting teeth, *Euparkeria* had many affinities with the first dinosaurs that arose in the Late Triassic. This slender-bodied reptile also had bony armored scales on its back—a trait seen, often in spectacular extremes, in some later archosaurs, including dinosaurs. *Euparkeria* had hind legs that were one-third longer than its front legs. This suggests that *Euparkeria* was a tiny powerhouse that sometimes could scamper on two feet— an early appearance of bipedalism, another trait later perfected by many kinds of dinosaurs.

By the Middle Triassic, after the establishment of basal archosaurs, two general trends took shape in the continued evolution of the archosaurs. The first trend was represented by the crurotarsans and included all archosaurs whose skeletal features were more like crocodylians than birds. In contrast, the creatures of the second trend—the ornithodirans—included all archosaurs whose skeletal features were more like birds than crocodylians. This seemingly simple distinction between the crurotarsans and the ornithodirans is based on the comparison of hundreds of data points related to the skeletal features of fossil specimens. A foundation of research

Euparkeria

such as this makes it easier for paleontologists to mark the evolutionary position of any newly discovered fossil reptile from the Mesozoic that might fall into one of these two important groups of archosaurs.

The Crurotarsi: Crocodiles and Their Relatives

True crocodylians first appeared in the Early Jurassic, but the line of crurotarsan archosaurs leading to the crocodylians included several diverse groups that lived during the Triassic Period. Of these, only basal crocodylomorphs—including a line of small to large, swiftly moving "proto-crocodylians" known as the sphenosuchians—survived the two mass-extinction events that closed the Triassic Period.

Crurotarsans arose during the Early Triassic; by the Middle Triassic, they dominated terrestrial ecosystems as the top predators. Some forms were also herbivorous. The crurotarsans diverged into several distinct lines of archosaurs, only one of which led directly to true crocodylians. All crurotarsans are united by a suite of anatomical features that hint at the ancestry of crocodylians: a heavily built skull, a long snout that narrowed near the end, conical or laterally compressed teeth, a short but muscular neck, and a long tail. Some crurotarsans had wide bodies and a sprawling posture, but some lines were more lightly built and nearly erect in their posture. A few converged on a body plan similar to that of theropod dinosaurs, with bipedal posture, long legs, and long necks. The backs of the crurotarsans often were armor plated, with rows of bony scutes reminiscent of today's crocodiles. The plant-eating varieties of crurotarsans were especially well protected; their backs and sides were thoroughly paved with tight-fitting rows of bony shingles, some of which bore spikes.

Fossils of crurotarsans have been found over a widespread geographic range, including Triassic rocks of North America (Arizona, New Mexico, North Carolina, and Texas); Europe (Scotland, Wales, Germany, Switzerland, and Italy); Central Asia (India); Africa (Morocco, Madagascar, and South Africa); South America (Argentina and Brazil); and possibly China and Thailand. The names of crurotarsans often contain the root word *suchus*, meaning "crocodile" in Greek. This attests to the crocodylian relationships of these archosaurs. An overview of the main groups of crurotarsans and their chief representatives follows.

Phytosaurs (Late Triassic Epoch). These were superficially crocodile-like archosaurs with long snouts and narrow jaws equipped with small, sharp teeth for snagging fish. Unlike true crocodylians, phytosaurs had nostrils on the tops of their skulls, just in front of the eyes, rather than at the end of the snout, and were not heavily armored. Well-known phytosaur specimens include *Parasuchus* (India), *Mystriosuchus* (Italy), and *Rutiodon* (Europe and North America), each of which was about 10 feet (3 m) long. Some specimens of *Rutiodon* have been reported that are considerably larger than this.

Ornithosuchians (Late Triassic Epoch). Superficially resembling carnivorous dinosaurs, the ornithosuchids had an erect posture and could have walked on their hind legs. Walking on all fours was probably their customary way of moving around, however. *Ornithosuchus* (Scotland), one of the best known members of this group, had a skull that is so strikingly similar to that of later dinosaurs that without any other skeletal evidence it would be difficult to prove that it actually belonged to a different line of archosaurs. The presence of armored, crocodilelike plates on its back; a short, flat pelvis that is weakly connected to its spine; and five toes on its hind feet instead of four clearly link it to the crurotarsans, however. This is not to dispute the dominance of these predators in the world of the Late Triassic, a time when the earliest dinosaurs probably were no match for such large and towering ornithosuchids as *Ornithosuchus* and *Riojasuchus* (Argentina). Both animals were up to 13 feet (4 m) long and weighed several tons.

Aetosaurs (Late Triassic Epoch). Among the first lines of herbivorous archosaurs was that of the aetosaurs. These small-headed, armor-plated animals superficially resembled the armored dinosaurs from the latter half of the Mesozoic. Aetosaurs had short, sprawling legs and stout bodies that were covered on the top, the sides, and sometimes on the bottom with a flexible grid of bony plates. For additional insurance against predators, some aetosaurs also had a series of short spikes around the perimeter of the torso. *Desmatosuchus* (Texas) measured about 16 feet (5 m) long and had two curved, hornlike spikes jutting to the sides from its shoulders. *Staganolepis* (Scotland, Brazil, Poland, New Mexico, Arizona, and Utah) was about 10 feet (3 m) long, with a long, broad body, a piglike snout, and a particularly heavy and deep armor-plated tail. Aetosaurs were equipped with peglike teeth for stripping greens from plant stems and roots.

Rauisuchians (Middle to Late Triassic Epoch). Perhaps the most formidable line of large predatory archosaurs were the rauisuchians. Primarily quadrupedal but capable of locomoting bipedally, the rauisuchians were among the largest carnivores that dominated in the second half of the Triassic Period. Think of them as crocodylians with shorter, rounder heads and a more upright stance that allowed them to run and chase down their prey. *Ticinosuchus* (Switzerland) was about 10 feet (3 m) long. Some other rauisuchians were smaller, with lighter-weight bodies and longer necks; among these were *Vytchegdosuchus* and *Dongusuchus,* from the Middle Triassic of Russia. The most characteristic members of this group, however, grew to proportions comparable to those of later mid- to large-sized dinosaurian predators. At about 30 feet (9 m) long, *Saurosuchus* was as large as another, less well-known rauisuchian, *Fasolasuchus* (Argentina), which may have been as long as 37 feet (11 m) and weighed 4 tons—true dinosaurian proportions. Remains of rauisuchians are widespread. In addition to those found in Argentina, Switzerland, and Russia, other important specimens have been discovered in Brazil (*Prestosuchus*); Germany and Poland (*Teratosaurus*); India (*Tikisuchus*); and the American Southwest (*Postosuchus*).

Crocodylomorpha (Late Triassic to present). Crocodylomorphs include the crocodylia and their extinct relatives. Subgroups within the crocodylomorphs include Eusuchia (including Crocodylia); Mesosuchia ("primitive crocodiles"); Protosuchia ("protocrocodiles"); and Thalattosuchia ("sea crocodiles"). The Crocodylia are restricted to only the living members of the crocodylomorphs and their immediate relatives.

The roots of the living Crocodylia date from the Middle Triassic and include some players that at first glance would not appear to be crocodylians at all. Some, such as *Gracilisuchus* (Middle Triassic, Argentina), were merely 12 inches (30 cm) long and may have walked on their slender **hind limbs**. The skull of *Gracilisuchus* had a mouth lined with small, pointed teeth and an overbite reminiscent of crocodylians. Another ancestral crocodylian from the Late Triassic of Wales was *Saltoposuchus*. This slender animal was even more lightly built than *Gracilisuchus*, although longer at about 1.6 feet (0.5 m) long. *Saltoposuchus* can be described as a slender, lizardlike animal with upright legs; these probably made it one of the swiftest crurotarsans.

Both *Gracilisuchus* and *Saltoposuchus* were most likely insect eaters, and it takes some imagination to picture them as being at the root of the crocodile family tree. What unites them with croco-dylians are the structures of their skulls, the vertebrae of the neck, and ankle structure. In the case of *Saltoposuchus*, its skull, although tiny, had begun to acquire traits that were recognizably crocodyl-ian: a long skull that was two-thirds snout and that was somewhat flattened on top, nostrils placed at the very front of the snout, and robust teeth in the upper jaw that overhung the lower jaw.

In 2003, paleontologist Hans Dieter-Sues reported the discovery of a new specimen of early crocodylomorph, this one from Late Triassic rocks of North Carolina. Named *Dromicosuchus* ("swift crocodile"), the animal was closely related to *Saltoposuchus* but was somewhat longer, at about 4 feet (1.2 m). Interestingly, this speci-men appears to have perished while struggling with a larger rauisu-chian archosaur whose bones were found on top of *Dromicosuchus*. Several missing neck bones and bite marks suggest that the larger reptile had taken a chunk out of *Dromicosuchus* before both were suddenly buried by a mudslide.

True crocodiles once were a more widely abundant and varied group than they are today. Although current crocodilians include the crocodiles, the alligators, the gavials, and the caimans, their numbers consist only of 8 genera and 21 species. The fossil record suggests that crocodylomorphs varied considerably during the Mesozoic and were found in many different habitats, not just in the tropical waters occupied by current species. In comparison with the 8 living genera, there are about 150 known genera of fossil crocodylomorphs.

One line of proto-crocodylians to survive the transition from the Late Triassic to the Early Jurassic was the group known as the sphenosuchians. Heavier and more crocodilelike than *Gracilisu-chus* and *Saltoposuchus*, this line is best represented by *Sphenosu-chus* (Early Jurassic, South Africa). One of the larger of the early crocodylomorphs, *Sphenosuchus* measured about 5 feet (1.4 m) long and has a skull that is more like the skulls of modern croco-dylians than were the skulls of other early members of this ancient

Protosuchus

clan. The sphenosuchians were widely distributed by the Late Triassic Epoch; similar forms are known from locations as widely separated as Texas and China.

Protosuchus ("first crocodile"), from the Early Jurassic of Arizona, is one of the best understood of the early crocodylomorphs. This animal is known from a nearly complete skeleton described by Edwin H. Colbert (1905–2001) and Charles Mook in 1951. *Protosuchus* measured about 3.5 feet (1 m) long and had many of the hallmark traits of crocodylians. The skull was not as long as those normally associated with crocodylians, but it was flat on top and had nostrils placed at the very end. The eyes were aimed outward and forward rather than mostly upward as in modern crocodylians. The front of the jaw featured a jutting **premaxilla**—the most forward portion of the upper jaw—with a battery of teeth; this is another trait that is seen in later crocodylians. *Protosuchus* was also preserved with significant evidence of body-armor plates on its back and stomach. It had more armor, in fact, than modern crocodylians, which suggests a strong carryover from the heavily armored anatomy of earlier archosaurs. The gait of *Protosuchus* was pictured by Colbert and Mook as somewhat more upright than that of modern crocodylians but nonetheless sprawling.

Ornithodira: Dinosaurs and Their Relatives

The ornithodirans are defined as the group containing the common ancestor of the pterosaurs and dinosaurs and all of its descendants. By the Early Jurassic Epoch, the ornithodirans were well on the way to becoming the dominant terrestrial vertebrates of the Mesozoic. Without the dinosaurs, the so-called "Age of Reptiles" may have become something entirely different—perhaps even an age of mammals. As the natural history of the Mesozoic Era unfolded, however, mammals continued to develop in the shadows of the dinosaurs until the course of evolution and a horrendous mass extinction removed the dinosaurs and pterosaurs from the picture, 65.5 million years ago. From the Late Triassic, when the earliest dinosaurs (as well as the first true mammals) first appeared, to the end of the Cretaceous Period, when they unceremoniously perished, dinosaurs and their closest kin ruled the planet. This rule lasted an astounding 162.5 million years and greatly influenced the course of evolution for other animals as well.

It is appropriate to take a closer look at the anatomy of the dinosaurs before delving into their origins and earliest representatives, the story of which occupies much of the rest of this book. As their namesake, "bird necks," suggests, one of these skeletal features is an S-curved or flexible neck. Other common features joining the pterosaurs and dinosaurs include an upright gait, a hingelike ankle joint, and the elongation and strengthening of the middle three toes on the hind limbs so that these animals could walk on them, rather than on the soles of the feet like other reptiles and many mammals. Birds, the living descendants of dinosaurs, share these same characteristics.

Defining Dinosaurs

Tyrannosaurus rex is arguably the best known dinosaur among the nonscientists of the world. It can be safely stated that the average six-year-old child knows more about *Tyrannosaurus* than he or she does about the president of the United States, the African lion, or the kinds of trees that grow in his or her neighborhood. The names of several other dinosaurs are almost equally familiar: *Triceratops*, *Apatosaurus*, *Stegosaurus*, *Ankylosaurus*, *Maiasaura*, and *Velociraptor* are among them. Ask any adult or child if he or she knows what a dinosaur is, and that person will answer with a confident yes.

Despite most people's familiarity with dinosaurs, there is much confusion over what a dinosaur is *not*. A dinosaur is not a water-dwelling animal, so plesiosaurs, mosasaurs, ichthyosaurs, and other monstrous marine reptiles do not qualify, despite the fact that they lived at the same time as dinosaurs. A dinosaur is not a flying animal, so pterosaurs, although closely related, are not dinosaurs. Picture books from one's youth may have confused dinosaurs with several other extinct vertebrates from entirely different times. The sail-backed *Dimetrodon* was a synapsid pelycosaur that lived long before the dinosaurs. *Dimetrodon* is more closely related to mammals than to dinosaurs. The wooly mammoth, though large and possibly cantankerous, is a mammal that lived at the same time as cave-dwelling humans, as recently as 10,000 years ago; it is not a dinosaur and it did not live alongside dinosaurs.

One must rely on the kinds of cladistic analysis described earlier to define the dinosaurs within the context of evolutionary relationships among vertebrates. As diapsid archosaurs of the group Ornithodira, the earliest dinosaurs shared with pterosaurs several anatomical features mentioned above: a flexible, curved neck; upright posture; an ankle joint; and elongate toes. Dinosaurs themselves are further united as a single clade by an additional suite of skeletal traits that differentiate them from other archosaurs. These include:

- An expanded **ilium**, the uppermost bone of the pelvis that is connected to the hip vertebrae, which contributed to the upright stance of the hind limbs.
- A distinct ball-and-socket structure connecting the upper leg bone (**femur**) with the hip joint; this made possible the upright stance of the hind limbs.

- Three or more fused **sacral vertebrae**, located just above the pelvis, that provided a strong, solid connection of the pelvic girdle to the hip vertebrae.
- A backward-facing shoulder joint that ensured an upright posture for the **forelimbs.**
- An elongated shelf or crest on the front edge of the upper bone of the forelimb (**humerus**) for the attachment of muscles.
- Three or fewer bones in the fourth finger of the forelimb.

Many of the special traits of dinosaurs are related to the development of an upright walking stance in which the legs fully support the weight of the body. Modifications to the shoulder girdle, forelimbs, hands, pelvic girdle, hind limbs, and feet all contributed to the improved mobility of dinosaurs and suggest that they had a more active, energetic lifestyle than did other kinds of reptiles.

Dinosaur Hips
The evolution of the upright posture in dinosaurs resulted in two distinctive styles of hips. These hip structures have been recognized since the 1880s as an important consideration in understanding the relationships between different kinds of dinosaurs.

Hip bones provide a point of connection to the trunk of the body for the hind limbs. The way in which bones and muscles are joined at the hip region has much to do with the posture and mobility of an animal. Hips of terrestrial animals consist of three basic parts, all of which enclose the **acetabulum,** or socket, to which the leg bones are connected. The broad, platterlike bone above the acetabulum is the ilium; it consists of two identical halves (ilia) connected on both sides of the spine to the fused, sacral vertebrae, as if cradling the backbone. Below the acetabulum on either side lie two longer bones known as the **pubis** and the **ischium**. The positioning of these three hip bones conforms to two general hip patterns seen in dinosaurs. In the first, called the saurischian, or "reptile" hip, the pubis points forward and the ischium points backward. In the second, called the ornithischian (or "bird" hip), both the pubis and the ischium point backward and lie parallel to one another. In the latter case, the pubis also has a forward-pointing extension called a **cranial process**. Note that despite its name, the ornithischian or bird-hipped dinosaurs are *not* the direct ancestors of birds; that distinction goes the saurischian dinosaurs, among which were meat-eating dinosaurs of all kinds and some of which later also evolved a backward-pointing pubis.

Hip structures add to the anatomical features that can be used to group different kinds of dinosaurs but barely hint at the diversity within this intriguing taxon of creatures. Within the saurischian dinosaurs can be found not only all of the carnivorous kinds of dinosaurs, big and small, but also the long-necked and most gigantic of the plant-eating dinosaurs. The ornithischians include only herbivorous dinosaurs, but these vary widely, from the largely bipedal duck-billed and bone-headed dinosaurs to armor-plated, horned, and plated quadrupeds.

The Changing History of Dinosaur Classification

Dinosaurs were not always considered to be a **monophyletic** group, or a single clade of animals descended from a common ancestor. A short history of their classification begins in 1842, when British paleontologist Richard Owen established the term *Dinosauria*—"terrible lizard"—to describe several puzzling specimens of extinct reptiles that previously had been described from fossils found in Great Britain and Germany. Owen recognized the animals as oversized reptiles but with limbs arranged in an upright, mammal-like posture for walking on land. Only a handful of such fossil specimens were known at the time, and all appeared to be from exceedingly large, quadrupedal animals. From the term *Dinosauria* comes the popular term "dinosaur."

There was a surge of fossil exploration following Owen's naming of the Dinosauria. Between 1842 and 1887, many noted fossil experts, including English naturalist Thomas Henry Huxley

Sir Richard Owen

(1825–1895) and Americans Edward Drinker Cope (1840–1897) and Othniel Charles Marsh (1831–1899), attempted through classification to bring clarity to the many varied kinds of dinosaurs specimens that were being discovered. By the 1880s, enough fossil evidence of dinosaurs had been unearthed for British paleontologist Harry Govier Seeley (1839–1909) to make a key observation: Dinosaurs appeared to be divided into two subgroups based on their hip structure. In 1887, Seeley divided all dinosaurs into these two groups, which he termed the Saurischia and the Ornithischia. Precious little fossil evidence about the origin of dinosaurs was available in Seeley's time. Because of this, Seeley believed that the two lines of dinosaurs were descended from different, rather than common, ancestors. He also believed that the leading candidates for these ancestors would be among the basal archosaurs, or "thecodonts" as they were known in Seeley's day. The implication was that dinosaurs were not a natural group of animals united by a common ancestor, but that they had two origins, one associated with each style of hip.

This idea stuck, and it remained in the mainstream of paleontological thought well into the second half of the twentieth century. By the early 1970s, however, continued analysis of the fossil record began to turn the tide toward the unification of dinosaurs as a single clade. In 1974, American paleontologist Robert Bakker (b. 1945) and British paleontologist Peter Galton published findings suggesting that dinosaurs were in fact a single natural group united by several skeletal, locomotor (related to limb structure), and metabolic traits. In 1979, noted British paleontologist Alan Charig (1927–1997), previously a stalwart supporter of the two-origins hypothesis, began to be swayed to this new way of thinking. He wrote, "There is no doubt that the Saurischia and the Ornithischia are related to each other, both being members of a larger assemblage (the archosaurs or 'ruling reptiles'); if we could go back far enough in time we should doubtless find that both groups were descended from the same ancestor, itself an archosaur." It was, however, Jacques Gauthier's spectacular achievement in cladistic analysis in

1986 that put the dispute to rest for the time being. In this landmark work of cladistic analysis, Gauthier identified more than 10 **derived** anatomical features that joined saurischian and ornithischian dinosaurs into a single group.

The practice of cladistic analysis has now become a well-established technique for analyzing the relationships between dinosaur groups. Computer software is commonly used to model data points in the analysis and to diagram dinosaur **phylogeny**, or family trees. For any current student of paleontology, the computer has become as necessary a tool for the study of dinosaurs as a rock hammer and hiking boots.

OTHER TRIASSIC DIAPSIDS

While the crurotarsans and ornithodirans had great success as part of the radiation of ruling archosaurian reptiles, several other kinds of diapsid reptiles became widespread during the Triassic Period.

A group of reptiles known as rhynchosaurs was one of the most common herbivore groups of the Late Triassic, particularly in South America and Africa. Neither lepidosauromorph nor mammal-like reptiles, the rhynchosaurs were distant kin of the archosaurs. The rhynchosaurs evolved independently of the true "ruling reptiles," however. *Hyperodapedon* was a small to medium-sized rhynchosaur that thrived on the tough vegetation of the Mesozoic woodlands. It walked on four squat legs and had a beaklike cutting surface as part of its upper front jaw. When viewed from above, the head of *Hyperodapedon* was triangular and showed the ample space devoted to batteries of grinding teeth in its expanded cheek regions. The success of this 4-foot (1.3-m) plant eater was due to its teeth and powerful beak and jaws, which could easily grind the tough, stringy vegetation of the time, including seed ferns. Fossils of *Hyperodapedon* are found in many widespread sites, including Brazil, Argentina, India, Madagascar, and Scotland. Unfortunately for the rhynchosaurs, however, climate changes by the end of the Triassic greatly diminished the abundance of seed ferns, and it appears that this line of diapsids became extinct because the animals were so specially adapted for

Hyperodapedon

Hyperodapedon fossil

this kind of food. During their time, however, rhynchosaurs such as *Hyperodapedon* were among the most populous vertebrates found in their habitats.

Another form of medium-sized herbivore of the Middle to Late Triassic was the trilophosaurids. The best known member of this taxon is *Trilophosaurus,* from the Late Triassic of Texas. *Trilophosaurus* had a lifestyle similar to that of the rhynchosaurs. *Trilophosaurus* measured about 6.5 feet (2 m) long and had a tall skull with small, rounded teeth lining the jaw in the cheek area; it lacked teeth in the front of the jaw, however. As in *Hyperodapedon,* the sturdy skull and jaw of *Trilophosaurus* were adapted to cut and chew the tough kinds of vegetation that were common in the animal's habitat. Curiously, *Trilophosaurus* did not have a lower temporal opening in its skull like other diapsids; this condition is believed to have evolved secondarily from an earlier skull structure that included the opening. *Trilophosaurus* had a sprawling posture, long digits reminiscent of modern reptiles, and a long, bony tail with stout chevrons along its **caudal** vertebrae.

One additional line of diapsids were the protorosaurs, a group with roots in the Permian that persisted into the Triassic. With long necks and lizardlike bodies, the group is best represented by the strange *Tanystropheus,* from the Middle Triassic of Israel, Italy, Germany, and Switzerland. *Tanystropheus* had a short body and a neck so long that it seems impractical. The animal was about ten feet (3 m) long, with six feet (2 m) of that length consisting of a long, stiff neck. The neck of *Tanystropheus* itself is a puzzle, being composed of only 10 elongate vertebrae and accounting for the meaning of its name: "long vertebrae." Because *Tanystropheus* was equipped with small, carnivorous teeth, many paleontologists assume that it lived in a near-shore environment, where it probably could take to the water to support its gawky body. One scenario pictures *Tany-stropheus* perched on a rock, dipping into the water below to catch fish and other small sea creatures. In fact, possible stomach contents discovered near the belly region of some specimens of *Tanystro-pheus* include fish scales and pieces of invertebrates. This suggests an aquatic or near-shore lifestyle. The feet of *Tanystropheus* were not webbed like those of most aquatic reptiles, however—a fact that adds to the puzzle of which environment is most appropriate for this enigmatic creature.

TRANSITION TO THE DINOSAURS

By the end of the Triassic Period, the aftermath of two major mass-extinction events had taken its toll on many once-prevalent lines of archosaurs. The only "ruling reptiles" to survive were the dinosaurs and crocodylomorphs, but their Late Triassic representatives were hardly rulers of their time. The extinction of other large carnivores and herbivores, however, provided an opportunity for the remaining archosaurs to diversify and expand their range. With the development of the dry but temperate Early Mesozoic climate and a widespread turnover in plant life from seedless forms to conifers, cycads, and ferns, dinosaurs proved to be especially adaptable. By the Early Jurassic Epoch, dinosaurs of various kinds were expanding rapidly to become the dominant carnivores and herbivores of the Mesozoic. Chapter 3 explores the origins of the dinosaurs and the reasons for their rapid rise to dominance of all terrestrial life.

SUMMARY

This chapter examined the roots, diversification, and relationships of the early archosaurs that led to the rise of the dinosaurs.

1. The three lines of early amniotes are differentiated by the number of temporal fenestrae in their skulls. They are the Anapsida (no temporal fenestrae), Synapsida (one temporal fenestra), and Diapsida (two temporal fenestrae).

2. Of these four groups, the Diapsida became the dominant vertebrate group of the Mesozoic and included the archosaurs, or "ruling reptiles," made up of dinosaurs, pterosaurs, crocodiles, and the dinosaurs' descendants, the birds.

3. Archosaurs diverged into two lines by the Middle Triassic: the Crurotarsi, including crocodylians and their extinct relatives, and the Ornithodira, including the pterosaurs, dinosaurs and their ancestors, and birds.

4. Dinosaurs are further defined by several special anatomical features. These include two different hip structures (saurischian and ornithischian); three or more fused sacral vertebrae; and hip and limb connections able to fully support the weight of the animal in an upright posture.

5. Dinosaurs are classified as a single natural group of animals descended from a common ancestral archosaur.

3

DINOSAUR ORIGINS

Tetrapod life of the Late Triassic was represented by large animals on land and in marine habitats. Aquatic predators—such as large-bodied amphibians and the 10-foot (3-m) long, crocodilelike phytosaur *Rutiodon,* found in Late Triassic rocks of Europe and North America—dominated the water. The most plentiful fossils of terrestrial faunas from the Late Triassic are those of plant-eating rhynchosaurs, diapsid archosauromorphs. Mixed among their fossils are those of less plentiful carnivores, including such large animals as *Ornithosuchus*, an ancestral member of the lineage that later diversified into true crocodylians.

Living among these creatures were the first dinosaurs. They were small-bodied predators and plant eaters that found an ecological niche and held tight in a world occupied by larger, more numerous vertebrates. The rise of the dinosaurs was certainly aided by a mass extinction that helped to wipe out their competition. Many scientists have postulated that competition from dinosaurs was a part of that extinction. The locations of the early dinosaurs coincided with those of the more dominant vertebrates of the time, and all of these creatures date to about 228 million years ago, at the transition from the Middle Triassic to the Late Triassic Epoch. The first appearance of dinosaurs in the fossil record is both sudden and widely distributed. Dinosaurs of the Late Triassic are known from five continents: the western United States of North America, Argentina and Brazil in South America, Morocco and Madagascar in Africa, Great Britain and Germany in Europe, and India in Asia—although India was not part of Asia in the Triassic. Even though the land areas where the early dinosaurs lived were still connected as parts of Pangaea, these places were still very far apart. The wide distribution of the first known dinosaurs suggests that they originated somewhat earlier, probably in the Middle Triassic Epoch; however, with currently known fossils, it is difficult to pinpoint where the dinosaurs may have originated.

This chapter explores the origins of the first dinosaurs, their rapid diversification, and reasons for their sudden prosperity in the fossil record.

ROOTS OF THE DINOSAURS

Dinosaurs as a group were tremendously varied. They included the largest known terrestrial carnivores and herbivores of all time as well as small, birdlike species. In between these extremes existed a wonderful menagerie of small, medium, and large dinosaurs that exhibited some of the most fanciful adaptations ever seen in vertebrates. Familiar to any fan of dinosaurs are examples of horns, crests, and other odd variations on headgear. Some dinosaurs are known for the sails on their backs or the defensive clubs and spikes on their tails. Dinosaurs came in bulky, armor-plated, tanklike models as well as sleek, speedy models with long, ostrichlike legs. All of these examples represent true dinosaurs, but not all of these kinds of dinosaurs existed at the same time. Nor did they all appear even in the early history of the evolution of the ornithodirans. The first wave of dinosaurs was much less varied. For their first 20 million years, dinosaurs slowly but steadily asserted their presence until, in the Early Jurassic Epoch, their numbers and diversity began to explode across the planet.

In their search for the origin of dinosaurs, paleontologists begin by making certain assumptions. First, because it is unlikely that a direct ancestor of dinosaurs ever will be found in the fossil record, scientists look for the next best thing: earlier creatures with features similar if not identical to those found in the first dinosaurs. Just what these ancestors may have been like is revealed by two pieces of evidence: the anatomy of the first known dinosaurs and a cladistic analysis of the specific traits that define them as dinosaurs.

The cladistic analysis provides a checklist of features that might be identified in any antecedent of the dinosaurs to which they might be closely related.

Another factor concerns the most likely places to find fossils of dinosaur ancestors. The search does not begin just anywhere, but by exploring certain kinds of rock formations already known to produce fossils of terrestrial organisms that occurred just before the earliest known dinosaurs. The earliest known dinosaurs are found in rocks that date from the earliest part of the Late Triassic Epoch, about 228 million years ago. To find the ancestors of dinosaurs, paleontologists begin by looking in rocks from the latter part of the Middle Triassic. One of the most productive localities for fossil strata of this age is found in northwestern Argentina.

Dinosaur Ancestors

The beginning of the Mesozoic Era was a time of upheaval for many tetrapod orders. Some 90 percent of all tetrapod species had become extinct at the end of the Permian Period. Among the reptilian survivors to cross over from the Permian to the Triassic were representatives of the diapsid "proto-archosaurs," such as *Proterosuchus* and *Erythrosuchus* from South Africa. These animals were moderately large at about 6.5 feet (2 m) long and were likely the most dominant predatory animals in their habitats. The body plans of *Proterosuchus* and *Erythrosuchus* were similar; each had a moderately long, crocodilelike body; short legs; a long skull; and jaws equipped with conical teeth suited for crunching fish and other small vertebrates. *Eryhthrosuchus* had a somewhat more upright posture than *Proterosuchus*, suggesting that it was a better runner and more adept at chasing down prey on land.

The earliest known dinosaurs appeared more than 20 million years after *Proterosuchus* and its closest kin. These earliest dinosaurs were small to medium-sized bipedal carnivores. They measured from 3 to 20 feet (1 to 6 m) long and were about as different in size and stature from *Proterosuchus* as a bald eagle is from a crocodile. Paleontologists therefore understand that there were several important intermediate evolutionary steps between the early "proto-archosaurs" and dinosaurs, and several additional fossil specimens from the Early and Middle Triassic provide insight into this transition.

The small "proto-archosaur" *Euparkeria* dates from the borderline between the Early and Middle Triassic Epochs and suggests that a remarkable transformation was under way in archosaurian evolution. The body of this small creature was about cat size. Its total length, including its tail, may have measured only about 3 feet (1 m) long, making it much smaller than its crocodilelike kin. Known from 10 specimens found in South Africa, *Euparkeria* had a more lightly built skeleton and skull than the proterosuchids. Instead of having the conical-shaped teeth of earlier archosaurian predators, *Euparkeria* was equipped with small, serrated and curved meat-eating teeth much more like those found in dinosaurs. The hind limbs of *Euparkeria* were longer and stronger than its forelimbs, suggesting that *Euparkeria* sometimes moved about on two feet, but it was predominantly quadrupedal.

In 2003, an archosaur similar to *Euparkeria* was described from Poland, extending the range of this important **transitional** line of diapsids to the Northern Hemisphere. Named *Osmolskina* after famed Polish paleontologist Halszka Osmólska, this animal was somewhat smaller than *Euparkeria* and dates from the end of the Early Triassic Epoch.

Moving geographically from South Africa and Poland, the next important archosaurs close to the lineage of dinosaurs have been found in rocks that date from the Middle Triassic of Argentina. *Lagerpeton* and *Marasuchus* are known only from partial skeletons but were clearly small, dinosaurlike, bipedal predators.

Marasuchus ("rabbit crocodile") is known from more complete fossil remains than *Lagerpeton*. The name *Marasuchus* refers to a superficially rabbitlike mammal of South America, called the mara, that can be found living today near the fossil site in Argentina. Superficially, *Marasuchus* looked much like the first known carnivorous dinosaurs. It had long hind limbs; two fused vertebrae at the connection with the pelvis (dinosaurs had three or more fused vertebrae at this juncture); a flexible neck that was probably S-curved; and flexible limb connections that improved its upright posture and mobility. Traits that separate *Marasuchus* from dinosaurs include an extra-long tail and other derived shapes of its vertebrae, pelvic bones, and leg bones.

Lagerpeton was less dinosaurlike than *Marasuchus*. Paleontologist Paul Sereno, who described *Lagerpeton* in 1993 with Argentine scientist Andrea Arcucci, noted that the feet of the animal had only two prominent, weight-bearing toes, with a third toe present but not long enough to be functional as *Lagerpeton* walked or ran. This trait, plus some unusual muscle scars on its limbs, suggested that *Lagerpeton* may have moved about using a rabbitlike hop.

Unlike *Euparkeria*, *Lagerpeton* and *Marasuchus* were close enough to being dinosaurs to place them within the archosaur group known as ornithodirans. So close to dinosaurs was *Marasuchus*, in fact, that it has become the earliest fossil to be designated as a dinosauriform, a member of a clade or group of ornithodirans (Dinosauriformes) that includes all taxa more closely related to dinosaurs than to pterosaurs. This does not make *Marasuchus* a dinosaur, however, because it possessed some anatomical features that clearly made it different. *Marasuchus* was part of a separate lineage of ornithodirans that diverged from a common ancestor it shared with true dinosaurs.

THE EARLIEST DINOSAURS

Dinosaurs made their first appearance in the fossil record in the earliest part of the Late Triassic Epoch. While a few of these early dinosaurs are known from excellent fossils, many are only understood on the basis of fragmentary remains. The complete story of early dinosaurs is woefully incomplete in most cases. Even the partial record of early dinosaurs shows that they existed at about the same time in several widely separated locations around the world, however; these locations include what are now Brazil, the United States (New Mexico and Texas), and India. Having become widely distributed by the Late Triassic suggests that the dinosaurs currently recognized as being the first were the descendants of even older dinosaurs yet to be discovered.

If a paleontologist were to bet on the most likely location in which to find additional clues about the origins of dinosaurs, a good place to start would be South America because that is where the earliest remains currently known are found. *Staurikosaurus* ("lizard of the Southern Cross"), from Brazil, dates from the earliest part of the Late Triassic, about 228 million years ago. First described in 1970 by Edwin Colbert, *Staurikosaurus* is known only from a partial skeleton and lower jaw, but the features exhibited by its backbone, pelvis, and jaw clearly identify it as a true dinosaur. *Staurikosaurus* measured about 6 feet (2 m) long and probably weighed about as much as a medium-sized dog. It had a sliding joint in its lower jaw—the intramandibular joint—that allowed the part of the jaw that contained its teeth to move forward and backward, making it more difficult for prey to wriggle free.

Two additional small to medium-sized carnivorous dinosaurs from the Early Triassic have been found in Argentina, *Eoraptor* and *Herrerasaurus*. Both are known from excellent skeletons. *Eoraptor* ("dawn thief") was the smaller of the two; it measured a mere 3 feet (1 m) long and had a lightweight body. At up to 15 feet (5 m) long, *Herrerasaurus* was the larger of the two. It was named after Victorino Herrera, the Argentine goatherd who found the first specimen in 1963. The evolutionary position of *Herrerasaurus* was not well understood until the 1990s, when additional specimens were studied.

All three of these early carnivores exemplified the body plan from which all other dinosaur body plans appear to have evolved for more than 160 million years. They had long hind limbs to provide mobility; a center of gravity near the hips, so that the animal could

Staurikosaurus

easily lean over to maintain a balanced gait while running; flexible arms for grasping prey; a short body; a flexible, S-curved neck; and a long tail for additional balance.

Staurikosaurus, *Eoraptor*, and *Herrerasaurus* were all "lizard-hipped" saurischians, one of the two main types of dinosaurs based on hip design. As a group, these three dinosaurs are classed as *basal saurischians*, a primitive group of saurischians that preceded the radiation of more advanced and closely related carnivorous dinosaurs.

The "lizard-hipped" dinosaurs were not limited to carnivores, and the first evidence of plant-eating saurischians also dates from the early part of the Late Triassic. These herbivores were the "prosauropods," an early group of long-necked, plant-eating dinosaurs that appear in the fossil record only slightly later than the *Staurikosaurus*, *Eoraptor*, and *Herrerasaurus*. One of the earliest of these is

Eoraptor

Saturnalia (Brazil), which is known from three partial skeletons and measured about 6 feet (1.75 m) long, a medium-sized animal within its domain. *Saturnalia* lived at roughly the same time as the earliest known carnivores of Argentina.

The roots of "prosauropods" are somewhat obscure. In 1999, two incomplete specimens of a saurischian from Brazil was discovered that might provide a common link between the "prosauropods" and theropods. *Guaibasaurus* dates from approximately the same time as *Herrerasaurus* but appears to have been more primitive in such skeletal features as its dorsal vertebrae, pelvis, upper leg bone (femur), and foot, giving it some close similarities to "prosauropods." *Guaibasaurus* may in fact represent a common ancestor to both theropod and "prosauropods."

"Prosauropods" were plentiful by the end of the Triassic. They grew large and bulky, sometimes exceeding 33 feet (10 m) in length—a clear sign of the **gigantism** to come in succeeding lines of dinosaurian herbivores. "Prosauropod" remains are plentiful and found in all corners of the world—including Germany, Argentina, South Africa, Lesotho, Zimbabwe, China, England, and Antarctica—but, strangely, not in the American Southwest. They

Herrerasaurus

are among the best known of the Triassic dinosaurs and were certainly abundant.

Dinosaurs of the Late Triassic are not limited to those with saurischian hips. One basal member of the Ornithischia, the plant-eater *Pisanosaurus*, was discovered in the same rock formation that yielded fossils of *Herrerasaurus* and *Eoraptor*. Known only from a fragmentary skull and skeleton, *Pisanosaurus* includes traits that connect it with later ornithischians, but its lineage remains somewhat clouded by a lack of diagnostic evidence. Even so, this small dinosaur, measuring perhaps 3.3 feet (1 m) long, clearly lived alongside the first known predatory dinosaurs. This suggests that larger carnivores such as *Herrerasaurus* may have fed on this herbivore. Only a few small ornithischian dinosaurs are known from the Late Triassic. Yet from this tiny handful of taxa, they would later eventually develop into many diverse lines of plant eaters, including armored and plated dinosaurs, iguanodonts, "duck-bills," and the horned dinosaurs.

(continues on page 62)

THINK ABOUT IT

The Search for the Earliest Dinosaurs

Several generations of the world's most prominent paleontologists have been engaged in the search for dinosaur beginnings. Discoveries made over many decades have gradually improved our knowledge of the first dinosaurs.

Hermann von Meyer (1801–1869) was a German naturalist and fossil hunter during the formative years of dinosaur science. His most celebrated fossil was that of the bird-reptile *Archaeopteryx* that he described in 1861. Long before then, however, he had been working in the fossil beds of southern Germany, where a rich fauna of terrestrial life was recorded. In 1837, several years before the word "dinosaur" was coined by Richard Owen, von Meyer had come across some large, stocky bones and given them the name *Plateosaurus*, or "flat lizard," to describe what was clearly a large, bulky animal. The original specimen was not complete and consisted primarily of limbs, vertebrae, some digits, and a fragmentary skull. Without a complete pelvic girdle or teeth, the true affinities of the "gigantic saurian" were not clear. A complete understanding of *Plateosaurus* did not come for another 84 years, until another German paleontologist, Friedrich von Huene (1875–1969), completed his own landmark study. Von Huene had recovered thousands of bones, making up several complete skeletons of *Plateosaurus,* from a wooded hillside near Trossingen, Germany. What was revealed in these bones was a large, bulky, plant-eating dinosaur that measured almost 30 feet (9 m) long, with a small head affixed to a moderately long neck, a stout body, and a long, heavy tail. Von Huene's famous paper describing *Plateosaurus* made him something of an international star among fossil hunters. The energetic German continued to work well into his eighties and named more new dinosaurs than any other paleontologist before or during his time.

The discovery and understanding of the first carnivorous dinosaurs in Argentina is another story that involved decades of detective work. In 1959, Argentine paleontologist Osvaldo Reig (1929–1992) explored the badlands of the Ischigualasto region of northwest Argentina with his guide, a local artisan and goatherd named Don Victorino Herrera. The region contained rocks dating from the earliest part of the Late Triassic Epoch, and from these he described *Herrerasaurus*, a sizable predatory dinosaur, based on some fragmentary limbs, pelvic elements, and vertebrae. From these rocks, Reig described *Herrerasaurus*, a sizable predatory dinosaur. He based his description on some fragmentary limb, pelvic, and vertebrae elements. The discovery was significant because it pushed back the origin of dinosaurs even further than *Plateosaurus*, but the fossil material was incomplete and left many unanswered questions about the evolutionary position of *Herrerasaurus*.

Plateosaurus

The fossil location that yielded *Herrerasaurus* was visited by some of the most famous paleontologists of the twentieth century, including von Huene in 1930 and Alfred Romer in 1958. But it was 30 years later before significant new fossils of *Herrerasaurus* were unearthed. In 1988, American paleontologist Paul Sereno mounted an eight-week expedition to the Ischigualasto region to search for more fossils of early dinosaurs. This was Sereno's first expedition as a leader. He was joined by Argentine

(continues)

(continued)

colleagues, including the legendary paleontologist José Bonaparte (b. 1928), whose numerous discoveries span the entire duration of the dinosaur age, and Fernando Novas. Since that time, Sereno and Novas have become two of the superstars of dinosaur science; in 1988, however, Sereno in particular was still trying to make his mark in the field.

Three weeks into the expedition, Sereno made the discovery of a lifetime, an **articulated** skeleton of *Herrerasaurus* eroding out of the dry badland sandstone. Sereno immediately understood the significance of the find. "Unlike the early finds reported 25 years before," explais Sereno, "this skeleton had a skull and forelimbs, which allowed the first accurate reconstruction of this very primitive dinosaur." The specimen included the first skull found for *Herrerasaurus*; in subsequent expeditions, Sereno's team found several other partial skeletons. Sereno and Novas went on to describe the spectacular fossil and also had another surprise up their sleeves. In 1991, during one of their follow-up expeditions to the same territory, expedition member Ricardo Martinez of Argentina discovered the remains of a contemporary of *Herrerasaurus*, the 3-foot (1-m) long *Eoraptor*.

Here is one footnote to the *Herrerasaurus* story. Recall that the dinosaur was originally named by Reig in 1963 after Don Victorino Herrera, the local man who led Reig to the site. Sereno had the chance to meet Herrera and his wife, still living in their humble village home at the foothills of the Andes mountains, just after Serano's discovery of the new specimen of *Herrerasaurus*. Herrera died in 1990.

(continued from page 59)

Unambiguous evidence of the first dinosaurs from the Late Triassic paints a picture of a world already populated with a variety of these creatures. These early dinosaurs were outnumbered by other kinds of reptiles and mammal-like reptiles; the presence of dinosaurs in the fossil record increases dramatically toward the end of the Triassic. This clearly shows that their fortunes had turned, and the world was falling under the control of the ruling reptiles. How this transition occurred is the subject of the discussion below.

RISE OF THE DINOSAURS: GOOD FORTUNE, OR BETTER GENES?

Before the first dinosaurs, terrestrial life during the first half of the Triassic Period was dominated by several other kinds of reptiles and synapsids. *Lystrosaurus*, a pig-sized plant eater, and its dicynodont kin were the most common herbivores. The role of predator was aptly filled by numerous kinds of cynodonts, ancestors of modern mammals, as well as a growing number of "proto-archosaurs." Most cynodonts were dog-size, and some, such as *Cynognathus*, had long canine teeth for stabbing prey. By the Middle and Late Triassic, larger and more formidable herbivores and carnivores were widely distributed, including the bulky, armor-plated, plant-eating aetosaurs; huge predatory rauisuchians such as *Saurosuchus*; and early members of the crocodylomorph group. Yet the reign of the **therapsids** and reptiles such as the rhynchosaurs was short-lived, and they soon were supplanted entirely by archosaurs, especially the dinosaurs.

The changeover from therapsids and pre-dinosaurian archosaurs to dinosaurs was geologically rapid. By the end of the Triassic, dinosaurs, pterosaurs, and their crocodylomorph kin had become the dominant terrestrial life-forms. Their reign lasted until the end of the Mesozoic Era, a total of about 160 million years.

Scientists have been debating for many years just how the dinosaurs assumed their role as the most dominant land vertebrates of the Mesozoic Era. Two theories have been proposed to explain the rapid radiation of the dinosaurs in the Late Triassic. The older, more traditional view has been that dinosaurs were better equipped anatomically to compete for their place in the habitat. This is the "evolve or die" hypothesis, explained by British paleontologist Alan Charig in the 1980s. The other theory, strongly supported by British paleontologist Michael Benton (b. 1956), is that dinosaurs were simply in the right place at the right time, filling ecospaces conveniently vacated by the extinction of other prominent vertebrate groups.

Evolve or Die

According to the competitive, or "evolve or die," point of view, the "thecodont" ancestors of archosaurs, and then the archosaurs themselves, developed certain physical characteristics that made them superior at hunting prey. In other words, archosaurs had superior genes that led to the evolution of advantageous traits. Chief among these traits was an upright posture. Charig colorfully pictured a Middle Triassic world in which "thecodonts," with their upright gait, could dominate other reptile groups like never before. "Other carnivores," wrote Charig, in his 1983 book *A New Look At the Dinosaurs*, "found themselves competing unsuccessfully with the great thecodontians for the diminishing supplies of meat, and herbivores were harried without respite; indeed, the great carnivorous thecodontians were such successful predators that they eventually brought about the decline and extinction of the animals on which they preyed and likewise of the other carnivores with which they were competing." Charig thought that dinosaurs had a competitive edge over other animals and viewed their rise as a case of faunal replacement in which dinosaurs simply outdid other kinds of animals.

American paleontologist Robert Bakker, also studying this matter in the 1980s, agreed with the "evolve or die" hypothesis and offered a new twist to the idea. He suggested that dinosaurs were endothermic creatures, warm-blooded and able to generate their own body heat internally, like mammals. If this were so, warm-bloodedness resulted in dinosaurs that were more continually active, day and night, than their ectothermic, or cold-blooded, contemporaries. This warm-bloodedness possibly made the dinosaurs faster and better competitors. One of the difficulties with Bakker's theory of dinosaur endothermy is that it cannot be positively proved, especially for the earliest of this line of animals. Studies of later dinosaurs and their rapid growth patterns have strongly suggested that dinosaurs had a high-energy metabolism for at least part of their lives, but many factors in addition to endothermy can contribute to such a metabolism.

At the heart of the "evolve or die" hypothesis is that early archosaurs and dinosaurs gained their advantage over dicynodonts and other mammal-like reptiles, large-bodied amphibians, rhynchosaurs, and other well-established reptilian groups over a long period spanning perhaps 45 million years of the Middle and Late Triassic Epochs. Opponents of this theory, led and inspired by Michael Benton and his work, have mounted several important arguments against the idea of gradual faunal replacement as the key to early dinosaur success.

In the Right Place at the Right Time

Michael Benton first opposed the "evolve or die" hypothesis of early dinosaur radiation in the early 1980s as a consequence of his own research into mass-extinction events. He found that the changeover from nondinosaurs to dinosaurs in the Late Triassic was not gradual, but sudden. Additional work on quantifying the effects of Late Triassic mass extinctions by Benton and others concluded that there were two successive mass-extinction events during the Late Triassic that wiped out large numbers of terrestrial animals and caused a widespread transformation of flora.

Accumulating fossil evidence clearly shows that dinosaurs benefited from the disappearance of other, previously dominating reptilian lines of their day. According to Benton, the earliest dinosaurs from about 228 million years ago made up only 1 percent to 2 percent of individuals found in fossil records of that time. A mass-extinction event about 225 million years ago decimated most of the cynodonts, dicynodonts, and rhynchosaurs. Following this extinction event, dinosaurs represented 50 percent to 90 percent of all individual fossils found in those deposits, a rapid and undeniably dramatic increase in their radiation and diversity. This evidence clearly casts aside Charig's theory that the rise of the dinosaurs was achieved slowly as they outcompeted their Late Triassic rivals.

Instead, dinosaurs simply moved in and prospered in ecospaces left vacant by extinctions.

Additional evidence strongly supports the idea that the success of the early dinosaurs was due to their good fortune rather than to an inherent competitive edge. Anatomical adaptations such as an upright gait are no longer viewed as exclusively archosaurian. Several other kinds of Triassic reptiles developed erect or semierect gaits, and yet they, too, were wiped out. Bakker's warm-bloodedness theory cannot be positively proved from the fossil record. There also was a rapid changeover in climate at the end of the Triassic—an aftereffect of the mass extinctions. The first dinosaurs arose in areas where some of these climatic changes were most profound, producing a drier and warmer habitat. A rapid changeover in flora to a conifer-dominated world also worked to the advantage of dinosaurs because it killed off herbivores that were best adapted for the kinds of plants typical of the old climate. Dinosaurs became well adapted for eating hard, tough vegetation—such as horsetails, ferns, and conifers—that was prominent all over the world.

After gaining a toehold in the Late Triassic Epoch, dinosaurs diversified rapidly and began to spread across the globe. With the extinction of other previously dominant groups of herbivores (rhynchosaurs, dicynodonts) and carnivores (phytosaurs, rauisuchians) by the end of the Triassic, plant-eating and meat-eating dinosaurs quickly took over their niches and evolved several large-bodied forms. Both saurischian and ornithischian dinosaurs were well-positioned by the end of the Triassic to expand still further into the enormous variety of dinosaurs that have become known. Chapter 4 provides an overview of the evolutionary tree of dinosaurs and takes a closer look at the early saurischians.

DINOSAUR DIVERSITY AND RELATIONSHIPS

Dinosaurs were a monophyletic, or natural, group of archosaurs descended from a common ancestor. From that early archosaurian stock, the first dinosaurs quickly diverged into two large groups based on the structure of the pelvic region: those with saurischian,

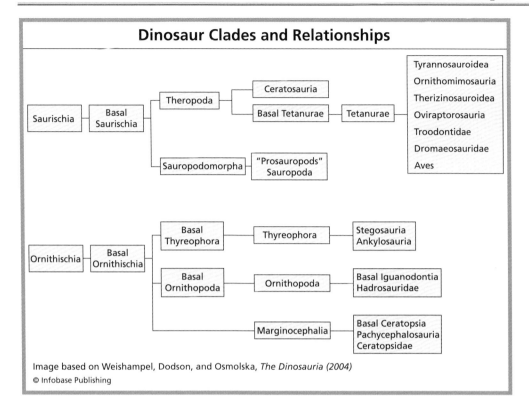

Dinosaur Clades and Relationships

Image based on Weishampel, Dodson, and Osmolska, *The Dinosauria (2004)*
© Infobase Publishing

or lizardlike, hips and those with ornithischian, or birdlike, hips. Within those two great divisions, dinosaurs further diversified in some astounding directions. This led to a collection of animals with an enormous range of sizes, body plans, and lifestyles. The variety of dinosaurs was staggering, even within similar groups. Carnivorous dinosaurs, for example, included at least nine distinguishable groups that ranged in size from creatures the size of a crow to some species that grew to more than 45 feet (13.5 m) in length. Sauropods, the long-necked plant eaters, are famous for representing the largest land animals ever to walk the Earth. One familiar sauropod is *Apatosaurus*, which weighed 20 tons and was 70 feet (21 m) long. Yet there was such a thing as a small sauropod as well, as represented by *Europasaurus,* a sauropod whose fossils were recently discovery in Germany. *Europasaurus* weighed only about a ton and was a mere 20 feet (6 m) long, including the tail, when fully grown. Compared to most of today's animals, *Europasaurus* was a large creature; it weighed about as much as a yak or a juvenile hippopotamus. By dinosaur standards, however, *Europasaurus* was a lightweight in the world of long-necked plant eaters.

It is important to view the major clades, or groupings, of dinosaurs to understand the broad variety of their forms and evolutionary relationships. The diagram Dinosaur Clades and Relationships serves as a guide to the major groups and evolutionary relationships of dinosaurs. This diagram introduces the names of dinosaur clades that will continue to be used throughout *Dawn of the Dinosaur Age*.

The next section of *Dawn of the Dinosaur Age* explores the early saurischian dinosaurs, early rulers of the dinosaur reign.

SUMMARY

This chapter explored the origins of the first dinosaurs, their rapid diversification, and the reasons for their sudden prosperity in the fossil record.

1. The earliest known dinosaurs are found in fossil deposits from the early part of the Late Triassic Epoch, about 228 million years ago.
2. Dinosaurs were already diverse and widespread by the Late Triassic, suggesting that their true origins date back to the Middle Triassic.
3. The small "proto-archosaur" *Euparkeria* dates from the borderline between the Early and Middle Triassic Epochs and appears to have been closely related to the ancestral roots of the dinosaurs.
4. *Lagerpeton* and *Marasuchus,* from the Middle Triassic Epoch, were early members of the archosaur group Ornithodira, the same group that includes dinosaurs and pterosaurs.
5. The first dinosaurs included the *Staurikosaurus* from Brazil and *Herrerasaurus* and *Eoraptor* from Argentina. They were predatory saurischian dinosaurs.

6. "Prosauropods" were large, saurischian herbivores from the Late Triassic Epoch, the first wave of important dinosaurian plant eaters.

7. *Pisanosaurus* is the earliest known ornithischian dinosaur and dates from the early Late Triassic of Argentina.

8. The rapid rise of the dinosaurs in the Late Triassic Epoch was likely due to their opportunistic expansion into ecological niches left vacant by the extinction of other, once-dominant vertebrates.

SECTION TWO:
DINOSAURS OF THE
EARLY MESOZOIC ERA

4

PREDATORY SAURISCHIAN DINOSAURS: THE THEROPODS

The best known of the earliest dinosaurs were small to medium-sized, bipedal predators that lived 228 million years ago, at the beginning of the Late Triassic Epoch. Before the end of the Triassic, these creatures were joined by the "prosauropods," a widespread group of large-bodied herbivores that represented a prototype for the giant, long-necked plant eaters to follow in the Jurassic Period. Both of these lines of dinosaurs were saurischians and had the characteristic "lizard hip" pelvis associated with this one of the two major group of dinosaurs.

There are two main branches on the family tree of saurischian dinosaurs. One branch, the **Theropoda**, includes all of the carnivorous dinosaurs. *Tyrannosaurus* was a saurischian theropod dinosaur, the "tyrant lizard king" of meat eaters and certainly the most famous dinosaur of all time. The other branch, the **Sauropodomorpha**, is made up of the "prosauropods" and sauropods, including the best-known giants of the dinosaur world, the earth-shaking, long-necked herbivores. *Apatosaurus*, the "deceptive lizard" once known as *Brontosaurus* ("thunder lizard"), was a member of the sauropod branch of saurischian dinosaurs. As different as they were, *Apatosaurus* and *Tyrannosaurus* were both part of the same group of dinosaurs that broke off from the other type—the ornithischians—early in the evolutionary history of the Dinosauria.

While the hip structures of the theropods and sauropodomorphs were similar, the two kinds of dinosaurs differed widely in most other respects, as exemplified by their different body plans and lifestyles. This chapter introduces early theropods and sauropodomorphs that flourished during the Late Triassic and Early Jurassic Epochs.

THEROPODA: CARNIVOROUS DINOSAURS

All meat-eating dinosaurs, large or small, are members of the saurischian group Theropoda ("beast foot"). American paleontologist Othniel Charles Marsh coined the name "Theropoda" to differentiate the feet of carnivorous dinosaurs from those of various kinds of plant-eating dinosaurs. Marsh's interpretation of the word "beast" was not just any old beast, but a "beast of prey." This fact has been pointed out by Ben Creisler, an active expert on the derivation of dinosaur names. According to Creisler, by inferring the name "beast of prey," Marsh was highlighting one of the signature traits of all carnivorous dinosaurs: birdlike three-toed, clawed feet similar to those seen in modern birds of prey.

The scientific classification of theropods has been updated many times in recent years due to increased knowledge about their diversity and traits. Until the 1980s, the traditional classification of theropods recognized only two main groups, based largely on size. The coelurosaurs included smaller, lightweight predators such as *Coelophysis* (Late Triassic, New Mexico) and *Ornitholestes* (Late Jurassic, Wyoming) whose size ostensibly increased only moderately over the course of the Mesozoic. The carnosaurs included the giant meat eaters such as *Allosaurus* (Late Jurassic, western North America) and *Tyrannosaurus* (Late Cretaceous, western North America) that could weigh several tons and reach lengths of 40 or more feet (12 or more meters).

A surge in dinosaur discoveries during the past 20 years has added many new theropods to the mix as well as more specimens of previously known examples. Additional fossils equate to improved knowledge of the specific traits that made each kind of theropod unique. By applying cladistic analysis to this new information, paleontologists—including Jacques Gauthier, Paul Sereno, Thomas

Holtz, Michael Benton, and others—have devised several competing schemes for defining the evolutionary relationships of theropods. While each of these schemes can differ substantively at the taxonomic level for given kinds of dinosaurs, there is some general agreement among paleontologists regarding the following high-level clades of carnivorous dinosaurs. These categories are used in *Dawn of the Dinosaur Age* and in other books in the series *The Prehistoric Earth* to organize the discussion of theropods.

Ceratosauria (Late Triassic to Late Cretaceous Epoch). The most basal theropods. This clade includes *Coelophysis, Dilophosaurus, Ceratosaurus,* and others.

Tetanurae (Middle Jurassic to early Late Cretaceous Epoch). Tetanurans make up the largest group of predatory dinosaurs and include the most derived nonceratosaurian theropods. The basal, or least derived, tetanurans include some of the largest and smallest theropods, such as *Spinosaurus, Suchomimus, Allosaurus, Giganotosaurus, Carcharodontosaurus, Compsognathus,* and *Sinosauropteryx.* The most derived tetanurans span the middle of the Jurassic to the last days of the dinosaurs and include such taxa as *Tyrannosaurus, Archaeopteryx, Velociraptor, Troodon, Oviraptor, Beipiaosaurus,* and *Gallimimus,* among others.

Dawn of the Dinosaur Age will explore the first of these two groups, the Ceratosauria, which represented the first successful radiation of theropod dinosaurs.

THEROPOD TRAITS AND LIFESTYLE

About 40 percent of all known dinosaur taxa are theropods. The most basal members of the clade were among the first dinosaurs to walk the Earth. Nonavian theropods were also among the last dinosaurs to perish, their success spanning the entire age of dinosaurs. They are survived today by avian theropods, the birds.

Theropod remains have been found on every continent. These animals ranged in size from the tiniest of dinosaurs, the chicken-sized *Compsognathus,* to hulking monsters such as *Tyrannosaurus,*

Giganotosaurus ("gigantic southern lizard"), and *Carcharodontosau-rus* ("great white shark-toothed lizard"). In between these extremes were many wonderful varieties of the basic two-legged carnivorous dinosaur.

Theropods are united by a suite of shared anatomical features. Many of these traits can be linked to the driving force behind their existence: finding, attacking, and consuming other animals.

Some of the best clues to the predatory lifestyle of theropods are found in their skulls. The theropod skull was lightly built and had a somewhat loosely joined assemblage of bones. This structure provided flexibility to absorb the physical shock that came with biting and subduing wriggling prey. The jaw itself was constructed more firmly, especially the lower jaw, made up of several bones including the tooth-bearing dentary. A primitive feature of the jaw found in the basal saurischian *Herrerasaurus* was an intramandibular joint that allowed the jaw to slide back and forth. This allowed the animal to maintain a firm grip with its teeth. A similar sliding joint was present in the lower jaw of many later theropods, including such giants as *Allosaurus.*

Theropod skulls came in a variety of shapes and sizes that were adapted to the choice of carnivory of a given kind of prey. A large head with strong biting jaws was the customary arrangement of the meat eaters that probably fed on other large animals. Predators that probably fed on insects and smaller animals had tinier, more bird-like skulls. The theropod skull had large fenestrae that lightened its weight, and large orbits, or eye sockets, as well. The presence of these indicates superior eyesight for tracking and following prey. Good eyesight is, in fact, a natural adaptation for predators, and some theropods had exceptionally large eyes. Whereas herbivorous dinosaurs had smaller eyes on the sides of their heads—better for scanning wide areas all at once to watch for predators—some theropods, including the troodontids, had forward-looking eyes that provided overlapping, stereoscopic vision, like that of humans. The ability to focus both eyes on the prey target greatly improves the ability of a predator to chase down and capture a fast-moving, evasive prey animal.

Most theropods were equipped with a mouthful of pointed, bladelike, serrated teeth. The deeply-rooted teeth of the largest tyrannosaurs were banana-sized and sturdy, capable of crunching through bone. Such teeth represent the extreme end of dinosaur tooth design for a highly derived theropod, the last of its line. For tyrannosaurs, whose arms were quite short, the head and jaws became its primary tool for grappling with prey. The oversized head, stout teeth, and highly muscular neck and jaw design suggest that tyrannosaurs probably captured their prey by lunging at it with open jaws, possibly in ambush.

Most other theropod teeth were less robust and more knifelike than those of tyrannosaurs. Such teeth provided a means to slice through the flesh of the prey animal once it was subdued. This is evident in the dromaeosaurs—dog-sized, swiftly moving predators such as *Deinonychus* (Late Cretaceous, Montana) and *Velociraptor* (Late Cretaceous, central Asia). The teeth of the dromaeosaurs were small and serrated but could be yanked loose if the prey resisted strenuously. Instead of relying only on their teeth, the dromaeosaurs used a combination of sickle-like foot claws and hand claws to slash their victims into submission while chasing them down. They probably also used the claws as hooks to get them in close enough to bite out big chunks of the prey! Once the prey was adequately weakened and unable to resist, the teeth of the dromaeosaur took care of the business of eating.

There were also a few theropod taxa that had no teeth at all; instead, these theropods had only a horn-covered beak. It has been presumed that dinosaurs such as *Oviraptor* (Late Cretaceous, Mongolia) and the ostrich-like *Gallimimus* (Late Cretaceous, Mongolia), two kinds of toothless theropods, fed on small vertebrates, insects, or perhaps even small, freshwater mollusks and crustaceans. There is growing evidence that some forms of toothless theropods were herbivorous. Oviraptorosaurs such as *Caudipteryx* and ornithomimosaurs such as *Sinornithomimus* had gizzards full of gastroliths, indicating that they were at least largely, if not entirely, herbivorous, like modern birds with the same structures. Carnivorous birds lack such gizzards.

The theropod skull was lightweight, but it also was mobile. It had a flexible connection to the vertebrae of the neck. This connection allowed the dinosaur to rotate its head from side to side, gave it reach, and allowed it to move its head quickly and precisely as it thrust its jaws to grab at moving prey. A similar joint connects the skull and neck of modern birds. In most theropods, this mobility was aided by the relatively long and flexible S-shaped neck.

Other parts of the theropod skeleton were equally optimized for the animal's carnivorous lifestyle. The forelimbs of theropods were always shorter than the hind limbs. The proportions of the forelimbs to the hind limbs, the supporting bony structure of the foot, and evidence of theropod trackways clearly indicate that theropods were bipedal. This posture freed the forelimbs for other matters, such as grasping prey, and theropods evolved some effective adaptations for doing just that. The evolution of theropod forelimbs began with the development of longer digits in the first dinosaurs. The second digit, equivalent to the index finger in humans, was the longest of the fingers. Theropods in fact had the equivalents of the human thumb, index finger, and middle finger. Later theropods developed longer arms with flexible shoulders that could be twisted enough to allow these carnivores to lunge forward to snag prey. The most deadly forelimb innovation of all was the addition of large, curved claws to the fingers—a trait seen in most later theropods, regardless of body size. Interestingly, in some smaller theropods, the ability to sweep the forelimbs forward and backward with a circular motion would later become the adaptation of wings for flapping, an important stage before the appearance of powered flight in their descendants, the birds.

The hind limbs of theropods provided excellent balance on three clawed toes, the longest of which was the center one. Most theropods actually had four toes, all with claws, but one (the first toe) was small and not typically in contact with the ground. The hind limbs provided two advantages to these hunting animals: the ability to move swiftly to chase down prey, and the use of the feet as an aid while hunting and subduing prey. Theropod toe claws were robust but not generally sharp because they continually rubbed against the ground when the animal walked. Except in dromaeosaurs, the claws were not used as weapons so much as for holding down prey or anchoring a carcass. In dromaeosaurs, the second toe of each foot was sharp and retractable so that it could be raised off the ground when the animal walked. These claws were certainly used as weapons, although recent experiments show that the toe claw would have made a poor weapon for slashing and disemboweling prey. Instead, dromaeosaurs probably used this foot claw as a puncturing weapon, wounding prey by jabbing at such vulnerable spots as the jugular or carotid artery in the neck. Even though the claws of most theropods were not sharp like those of the dromaeosaurs, theropod legs were undoubtedly strong and capable of delivering powerful kicking blows, not unlike the kicks delivered by extant flightless birds such as the ostrich and emu. The upper leg bone, or femur, was bowed and shorter than the rest of the leg. These traits improved the running speed of theropods.

Dromaeosaurs may have had the most elegant of theropod weaponry. Their forelimbs and hind limbs combined to form an impressive arsenal. The three-clawed hand was equipped with sharply curved claws. The hand was attached to a flexible wrist, allowing the animal to grab and twist with the movements of the prey. It was the foot of the dromaeosaur, however, that bore the most effective device of all, a large, pointed, retractable claw on the second toe of each foot. The toe claw retracted up out of the way when the animal walked but could be flipped down, like an open switchblade knife, when the dromaeosaur was on the attack. Such an arsenal leaves little to the imagination. One of the larger dromaeosaurs was *Deinonychus*, named "terrible claw" after its formidable foot claw. Everything about its anatomy suggests that this dromaeosaur

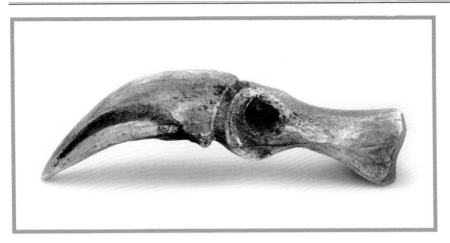

Forelimb claw of *Tyrannosaurus rex*

was an energetic, swift-running animal. After closing in on its prey—perhaps a moderately sized plant-eater such as *Tenontosaurus* (Early Cretaceous, Montana), which is also found in the same areas where the fossils of *Deinonychus* are found—the predator probably launched its attack by leaping at the victim feet first, with toe claws extended, gained a foothold on the prey, and punctured it with its claws. Thus did the bloodbath begin. The prey, weakened considerably, soon would be too weak to struggle. Using its forelimbs to hold the prey, *Deinonychus* could finish it off by biting and continuing to inflict puncture wounds with its feet.

Most theropods had long and somewhat stiff tails, a trait that improved their balance while running. The most reasonable way to envision a running theropod is to view it leaning forward, using its hip area as a fulcrum, with its head stretched out in front and its tail extended behind to maintain a counterbalanced posture and efficient forward motion. The posture of a running theropod may be compared to that of a racing cyclist who leans forward on dropped handlebars to improve the leverage and energy that can be applied to the pedals.

(continues on page 82)

THINK ABOUT IT

The Telltale Anatomy of Theropod Teeth

Is it possible to identify a dinosaur from its teeth alone? Can teeth be considered the "fingerprints" of an extinct species of dinosaur?

Vertebrate anatomy features two kinds of hard parts that make vertebrates unique among other organisms: bone and cartilage. Teeth are enamel-coated bone. Cartilage rarely fossilizes, so it does not help the paleontologist. Bone, of sufficient quality and quantity, can provide a highly accurate picture of an extinct animal and its lifestyle. When left with only fossil teeth, however, the paleontologist is much less able to ascertain the exact nature of an extinct animal, except at a most general level: whether it was a predator or a herbivore, for example.

For some kinds of fossil vertebrates, such as mammals, teeth were so highly specialized that they can serve as a means for identifying extinct taxa down to the species level. Mammals have **heterodont** dentition: different kinds of teeth in different zones of the jaws. Characteristics of the teeth are key to the adaptive strategy and success of a vertebrate and are passed along to its descendants through **natural selection**. The teeth of mammals are so informative that many clades of extinct mammals are first classified based on their dentition. A well-trained paleontologist, presented with only the teeth of an extinct mammal, will be able to identify which specific kind of mammal those teeth came from.

Most dinosaurs do not exhibit dramatic heterodonty in their dentition, which limits what can be discerned from a single tooth or part of a jaw bone. Being able to identify a dinosaur from little more than its teeth, however, would be a valuable tool for studying dinosaurs. Take the case of predatory dinosaurs. The teeth of theropods fossilized well and frequently are found in Mesozoic fossil beds that contain terrestrial specimens. Such teeth are often found to the exclusion of any other remains, suggesting that the teeth were shed by a living predator—not an uncommon occurrence because dinosaurs, like most reptiles, were able to replace a tooth whenever they lost one. Being able to identify the kind of dinosaur that shed such a tooth would enable a paleontologist to understand more about the range and interaction of a given taxon. Joshua Smith is an American paleontologist who believes that theropod teeth have more to tell science than what is obvious to the naked eye.

To find out whether the teeth of theropods are distinguishable from one another, Smith conducted an exhaustive, groundbreaking analysis of one well-known taxon, *Tyrannosaurus*. Smith suggested that if he could find traits in *T. rex* teeth that could distinguish them from the teeth of other theropods, then the same could be done for the teeth of other kinds of dinosaurs.

An experienced paleontologist can use the naked eye to gauge the relative girth, shape, and curvature of a tooth and then surmise with some accuracy the general size of the theropod whose tooth it is and the position of the tooth in the dental battery. The drawbacks to this approach are that eyeballing a specimen is a procedure that is prone to error, and the outcome is entirely dependent on the knowledge of the person doing the examination. To avoid such biases, Smith applied precise, electronically aided measurements and numerical analysis to measure such *T. rex* tooth data as size and spacing as well as morphological characteristics that included the curvature of the leading and trailing edges of a tooth, its length, its width, its breadth, its crown size and shape, the density of its serrated denticles, and other nearly microscopic traits of tooth structure. Once collected, such data can be objectively interpreted.

Smith examined and measured all the teeth of known *T. rex* specimens. Using methods that have been widely applied to the diverse morphology of mammalian teeth, Smith sought to determine whether he could extract data from the analysis of theropod teeth that would allow him to distinguish one taxon from another. Despite the superficially simple structure of theropod teeth, Smith's exhaustive research with *T. rex*

(continues)

(continued)

dentition demonstrated that this taxon of dinosaur could be singled out of the fossil record on the basis of its teeth alone. His work is of tremendous benefit to theropod researchers and to all dinosaur paleontologists who desire to create a gold standard for examining the teeth of any kind of dinosaur.

(continued from page 79)

Theropod Teeth and Feeding Styles

Dinosaur teeth, particularly those of theropods, are among the most common type of fossil found with the remains of these extinct creatures. The hard, enameled construction of teeth improved their chances of becoming fossilized, and some specimens still retain their original, enamel outer surface. Sometimes the only clue to the presence of a theropod is a tooth that it left behind. Fossil teeth have been found singly, without any other associated body parts, embedded in the bones of fossilized prey. Other teeth, most dramatically, have been found in association with the skull and jaws of a theropod fossil.

Teeth can be highly informative. In most cases, the general shape, size, and structure of a tooth immediately identifies its owner as being a carnivore or a herbivore. Pointed, serrated teeth are associated with carnivorous dinosaurs. Despite a superficial similarity in the shape and structure of theropod teeth among different taxa, closer examination can reveal subtle clues that disclose the kind of dinosaur that had a given tooth, its method of biting prey, and its eating habits.

Theropod teeth fall into three morphological categories, and each of these categories can be associated with a general group of predatory dinosaurs. The largest and most robust teeth were those of tyrannosaurs. The teeth of *T. rex* and its kin were as long and thick as bananas, deeply rooted, and sturdy enough to withstand contact with bones. Most other theropods had more bladelike teeth that were thinner and more razorlike than the teeth of tyrannosaurs. The third kind of theropod tooth was that of the spinosaurs, giant carnivores with gavial-like snouts. Spinosaur teeth were conical rather than bladelike, sharply pointed, and often not serrated.

The ways in which a theropod bites and uses its teeth are related to two aspects of the animal's anatomy and **physiology**: tooth design and **cranial** mechanics.

Tooth Design

Theropod teeth have been collected by paleontologists for nearly 200 years. The most typical theropod tooth had a slightly curved and pointed profile, with a bladelike shape and serrations on the forward and backward edges. Serrations consist of tiny undulations or bumps arranged in a tightly conforming row along the edge of the tooth. Serrations vary somewhat in shape from one kind of theropod to another, but most serrations are generally square and capped with tooth enamel.

The bladelike shape and serrated edges of theropod teeth led to a conventional view that they operated more or less like steak knives, slicing through the side of a prey animal with the ease of a knife through a juicy cut of meat. This view has changed since American researcher William Abler began examining the mechanical action behind serrated tooth designs. In 1992, Abler set out to take a close, comparative look at different kinds of theropod teeth to ascertain how they actually cut through meat. He did this by fashioning steel hacksaw blades to mimic a variety of serration patterns, in particular those of the giant carnivore *Tyrannosaurus* and the smaller, more ostrichlike *Troodon* (Late Cretaceous, western North America). Through his experiments, Abler identified two distinctive biting mechanisms at work in theropods with bladelike teeth.

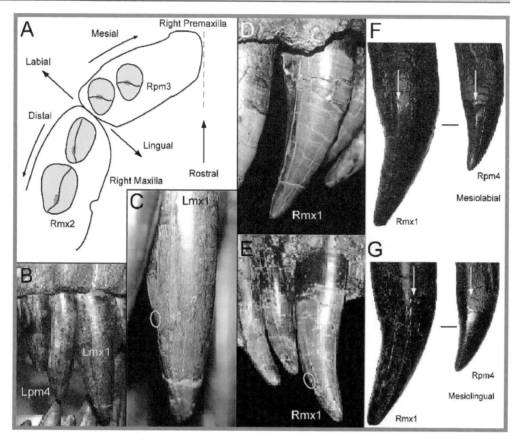

Shapes and structure of theropod teeth

The fat, robust teeth of *T. rex* had an innate gripping action associated with "tiny frictional vises" between neighboring serrations. The teeth of *T. rex* could not slice through meat with the ease of a sharp steak knife as once had been thought. Abler characterized the biting action of such robust teeth as a "grip and hold" action. *T. rex* muscled its way through dinner, grabbing, crushing, and tearing off chunks of meat. Theropods such as *Troodon*, with thinner, sharper, bladelike teeth, could more easily slice through meat using an action that Abler called "grip and rip"—an action more like that of the traditional steak knife.

Abler's examination of *T. rex* teeth revealed another surprise. The tiny gripping surfaces between the serrations of *T. rex* teeth were capable of snagging tiny fibers of meat that were difficult to remove. Abler speculated that the pockets trapped grease and spawned infectious bacteria on the biting edges of the teeth, essentially transforming the teeth of *T. rex* into a poison-tipped dental arsenal. An animal bitten by *T. rex* that escaped immediate death may have become sick enough from the toxic bite to weaken soon thereafter, while the lumbering *T. rex* followed not too far behind to finish it off. As speculative as this seems, a similar behavior is seen today in the Komodo dragon of Indonesia.

The Cranial Mechanics of Feeding Style

Abler's work on the innate cutting ability of serrated teeth was provocative. He reasoned that evolution produced teeth that were optimally designed for the lifestyle of a given dinosaur, and that understanding how the teeth worked could reveal aspects of a given theropod's lifestyle. This led to additional studies of theropods that modeled the action of the teeth within the context the animals' cranial mechanics.

Paleontologist Emily Rayfield of Cambridge University is a leading expert in the bite and stress forces that probably took place in the skull of a theropod when it fed. She has conducted noninvasive studies of fossil theropod skulls using computed tomography (CT) scans and engineering software normally applied to building mechanics. Using these technologies, Rayfield has been able to model the strong and weak points in various theropod skulls and suggest the ways the animals probably used their teeth when feeding. Her conclusions nicely dovetail with the tooth functions suggested by Abler.

Abler's "grip and hold" view of *T. rex* tooth design fits well with Rayfield's conclusion that tyrannosaurs used a "puncture and pull" technique when feeding. The big bite and bone-crushing teeth of *T. rex* would close on the prey and hold fast while the predator pulled back to rip off meat. A separate study by paleontologist Greg Erickson of the University of California, Berkeley, provided hard fossil evidence for the "puncture and pull" technique in the form of a *Triceratops* (Late Cretaceous, western North America) skeleton with bite marks that matched the puncture size of *T. rex* teeth.

In contrast to the "puncture and pull" technique was the feeding style of theropods with more slender, bladelike teeth, such as *Coelophysis* and *Allosaurus*. Rayfield's modeling of the skulls of those two theropods suggested that the power of the bite was focused at the front of the jaw, resulting in a "slash and tear" approach to feeding that reduced stress on the animals' teeth. In this scenario, a theropod would grip the prey with its front teeth and swing its head from side to side to rip off meat. This view fits nicely with the "grip and rip" tooth action described by Abler for this style of theropod tooth.

Theropod Courtship, Reproduction, and Parenting

The reproductive behavior of dinosaurs will never be fully understood because their fossil remains can only hint at the kinds of behavior that might have been natural for these extinct animals. There are no clear-cut anatomical clues for determining a dinosaur's gender that can be applied to every kind of dinosaur skeleton. Yet paleontologists remain fascinated with the family life of dinosaurs because of provocative fossil evidence about nesting behavior, parental care, and the growth of dinosaurs from hatchlings to adults. Understanding how these animals interacted to ensure the continuance of their species is an irresistible topic for those who try to paint the complete picture of dinosaurs as living creatures.

The fossil record may not shout out obvious answers about the reproductive behavior of dinosaurs, but it does provide clues. Another instructive source of information about dinosaur reproduction comes from observing living animals and inferring from their behaviors possible behaviors in dinosaurs. In the case of theropods, a suite of intriguing clues and assumptions is beginning to emerge that is helping scientists piece together an informed view of their courtship, reproductive, and parenting behaviors.

Courtship

Before two animals mate, they may partake in a ritual of courtship. During this time, a female is approached by one or more males from among which she chooses a mate. Whether or not dinosaurs behaved in this way cannot be known for sure, but it is reasonable to assume that some form of mating ritual took place. The motivation behind courtship and mate selection is most likely connected to an innate drive to propagate the species. Finding the healthiest or fittest mate available is a natural way to increase the likelihood that offspring will be equally healthy and will live long enough to mate and have offspring of their own. Such are the underlying instincts of all living organisms. We can safely assume that dinosaurs were equally motivated when it came to mate selection.

In the game of courtship, the first requirement for a male is to get the attention of a female. With modern birds, males generally are brightly colored, and females are not. This enables males and females to identify one another but may also give the advantage to a male with superior coloring. Just what a female bird makes of this male display is a matter of speculation. A more brightly colored bird may represent a healthier potential mate and a better chance for the continuance of the species. Or the bright colors may just happen to catch the female's eye. Whatever the case, a male bird's coloration is an example of an anatomically-based sexual-display feature.

When it comes to dinosaurs, the color of skin, hairlike filaments, feathers, and other possible nonskeletal elements of sexual display are not discernable from the fossil record. Fortunately, a variety of theropod skeletons exhibit bony anatomical features that may have served the purpose of attracting members of the opposite sex.

The variation between the males and females of a species is called **sexual dimorphism.** Such gender-specific features will be a recurring theme in the exploration of dinosaurs in this book and in other books of *The Prehistoric Earth* series. Differences between the sexes of a given dinosaur species are risky to assume with certainty unless a paleontologist is presented with a large number of specimens that most likely represent a random sampling of the

population and must surely include males and females. In later dinosaurs, such as the "duck-bill" dinosaurs (hadrosaurs) and horned dinosaurs (ceratopsians)—where dozens of specimens of some species can be compared—the size, shape, and presence of head crests and horns appear to signify male and female individuals. Using knowledge of living animals, paleontologists can assume that sexually dimorphic traits such as these probably were most prominent in dinosaurs that had attained reproductive maturity. This means that hatchlings and juveniles would display only the immature hints of such characteristics.

Anatomical features of theropods that may have been used for sexual display are mainly found on the head. The ceratosaur *Dilophosaurus* ("double-crested lizard")—perhaps best known for its wholly unsubstantiated portrayal in the movie *Jurassic Park* as having the ability to spit poison—was a 20-foot (6 m) long, Early Jurassic theropod from Arizona with a pair of prominent crests running the length of its skull. The crests were tall and thin and grew out of the bones at the top and front of the head. Because they were too weak to have been used for defensive purposes, American paleontologist Kenneth Carpenter surmises that the double crests would have been effective sexual-display devices, especially if the dinosaur turned sideways to give the appearance that its head was larger than it truly was. Other, less spectacular examples include the nose horn and short brow horns of *Ceratosaurus*, the short brow horns of *Allosaurus*, and the longer, jutting brow horns of *Carnotaurus*. Reinforcing the idea that nasal horns and brow horns were associated with mating and courtship is the possibility that they also could have been used in sparring contests between rival males—intraspecies battles intended to bruise but not kill the opponent.

Except for *Allosaurus*, the above cases for sexual dimorphism in theropods are not supported by an abundance of fossil specimens. Most of these dinosaurs are known from only a few good specimens—not enough to sample a species population accurately for males and females. A stronger case can be made for sexual dimorphism in two small theropods, *Coelophysis* (Late Triassic

Epoch, New Mexico) and *Syntarsus* (Early Jurassic, Arizona, South Africa, and Zimbabwe). Each has been found in **bone beds** that consist of many individual adults.

American paleontologist Edwin Colbert, who studied *Coelophysis*, and South African paleontologist Michael Raath, who did work on *Syntarsus,* each noticed that the adult specimens of these dinosaurs came in two basic forms. One form was more strongly built and had such features as a larger skull, a longer neck, more muscle scars around the elbow and hip, and stronger limbs. Scientists do not always agree, however, on how to tell the males from the females. In the case of *Coelophysis,* Colbert took a more traditional approach and believed that the larger, stronger individuals were males. In the case of *Syntarsus,* Raath came to the opposite conclusion and proposed that the females were the stronger, bigger-boned individuals, a variation that can be observed in modern predatory birds.

Working independently, paleontologist Kenneth Carpenter came to the same conclusion as Raath in regard to *Tyrannosaurus.* Carpenter believed that the larger, more robust form of *T. rex* was the female. The key to Carpenter's conclusion involved egg laying. Carpenter noticed that in larger *T. rex* specimens, the backward prong of the hip bone known as the ischium was angled downward in relation to the tail more than it was in *T. rex* specimens with the less robust body type. Carpenter reasoned that the increased space between the ischium and the tail provided a more ample path for the passage of eggs during egg laying. This same anatomical clue has been observed in some modern crocodylians.

Mating

Like other soft body parts, the reproductive organs of dinosaurs did not fossilize. To explain how dinosaurs mated is clearly a speculative venture, but it can be informed by the anatomy and behavior of the living archosaurian relatives of dinosaurs—birds and crocodylians.

It appears that all dinosaurs were oviparous, or egg laying, like extant crocodylians and birds. The study of dinosaurs is replete with excellent specimens of fossilized dinosaur eggs and nests. On rare occasions, the tiny remains of dinosaur embryos have been found inside fossilized eggs. In one remarkable find in 2005, an international team of paleontologists led by Tamaki Sato of the Canadian Museum of Nature found two shelled eggs in the pelvic region—right where the oviducts (egg passages) should be—of a small theropod dinosaur from China, thus providing direct evidence of egg laying in this type of dinosaur.

From an evolutionary standpoint, the anatomy and physiology of dinosaurs falls along a continuum that is closer to the crocodylians at one end and closer to birds at the other. This assumption can help us to understand the kinds of sex organs, or gonads, that dinosaurs possessed. More basal dinosaurs may have had gonads more like those of crocodylians. Those dinosaurs that were more closely related to birds—the later theropods—probably had sex organs most similar to those of birds. In dinosaurs, as in crocodylians and birds, eggs were probably fertilized internally.

Male crocodiles transfer sperm to the females by way of a penis. When not in use, the penis is tucked inside the body, behind an opening at the base of the tail called the *cloaca*. The female gonads, where eggs are produced, are located inside the female's body, behind a cloaca of her own. Similar anatomy was likely present in many dinosaurs.

Dinosaur Eggs and Nests

Today the study of dinosaur eggs and nests is a booming discipline within dinosaur science, but this was not always the case. Although paleontologists in the 1800s had recognized that dinosaurs were related to other reptiles and birds, nobody had discovered any remains of eggs or nests that were obviously dinosaurian. Some reports of fossil eggshells from France in the 1850s went largely unnoticed, and the fossil shells were attributed to extinct birds and crocodylians, not dinosaurs. Interest in dinosaur eggs changed dramatically between 1922 and 1925, when celebrity explorer Roy Chapman Andrews (1884–1960) led three fossil-hunting expeditions to central Asia for the American Museum of Natural History.

Roy Chapman Andrews

Although Andrews' original mission was to search for the fossil origins of humans, the area in Mongolia that he happened across dated from a much earlier time, the Late Cretaceous Epoch, when dinosaurs ruled. A few fragments of fossil eggshell were discovered at the end of the 1923 mission and assumed to be from birds. But

Walter Granger (1872–1941), the lead paleontologist of the expedition, was mindful that not much was known of fossil birds from that early a time. He suspected that the eggs might be dinosaurian in origin. Granger and Andrews found the proof they needed during the next expedition, in 1924, when they excavated fossil eggs in many locations. Some were fragmentary, some were complete, and some were still lying intact in what appeared to be nest **clutches**. It was the first definitive discovery of dinosaur eggs in close association with dinosaur skeletons. Discoveries of fossil eggs, nests, hatchlings, and rare, intact embryos of unhatched dinosaurs have grown dramatically since and have occurred on most continents.

Dinosaurs laid hard-shelled eggs that were more like those of birds than the soft-shelled eggs of crocodylians and other reptiles. The hard shell of the egg developed as the egg passed through the oviduct of the mother, where glands secreted a calcareous protective covering—the calcium-rich outer shell.

Preserved nests of dinosaurs show that they laid large numbers of eggs on the ground. Finding between 15 and 25 eggs in an intact nest is common; some fossil dinosaur nests included more than 40 eggs. The construction of the nest as well as the pattern for laying the eggs varied widely among different groups of dinosaurs. Nest construction was influenced by the materials available in the habitat to house the eggs. For example, the nest of the duck-billed dinosaur *Maiasaura* (Late Cretaceous, Montana) was formed from mud as a bowl-like mound. The nests then may have been covered by scraps of vegetation and mud to protect and encourage incubation of the eggs.

Dinosaurs laid their eggs in one of two basic patterns: groups of eggs called *clutches* and eggs laid in rows. The pattern of egg laying was probably most influenced by the size of the dinosaur. The largest dinosaurs, such as the sauropods, needed more room to lay their eggs and appear to have laid them in semicircular rows. Small to medium-sized dinosaurs preferred to lay their eggs in tight clutches.

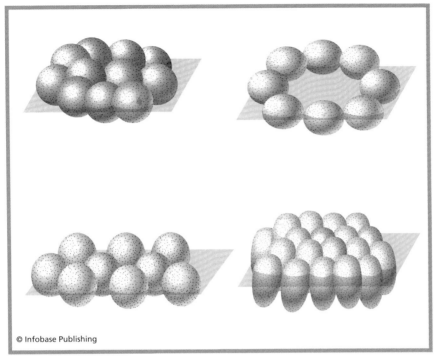

Clutch patterns of Asiatic dinosaur egg nests, including round, oval, and elongate-shaped eggs

The eggs that have been positively associated with the remains of theropods are elongate in shape and range from 5 to 21 inches (12 to 53.6 centimeters) long, depending on the taxon. These kinds of eggs have been found in Montana, Mongolia, and China. The largest dinosaur eggs currently known were laid by theropods.

Evidence concerning the nests of predatory dinosaurs is limited to a few celebrated cases. The fossil eggs discovered by Andrews and Granger in 1924 belonged to the small Mongolian theropod *Oviraptor*, although at the time they were thought to pertain to the horned dinosaur *Protoceratops*. This toothless predator laid its elongate eggs in a ring within a shallow nesting pit that it dug out of the sandy soil where it lived. *Oviraptor* nests contained up to 24 eggs; the eggs were arranged in a circle and rested slightly upright. The ring pattern was similar to that seen in brooding birds. A variation on

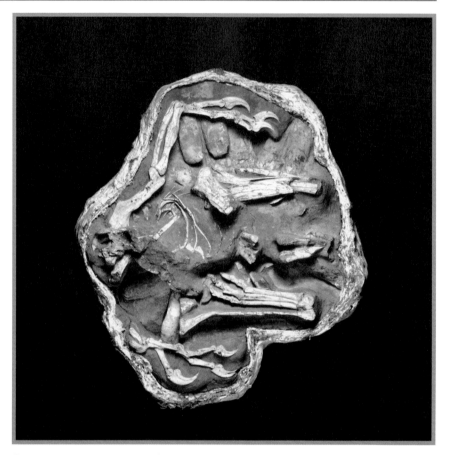

Oviraptor nest and eggs with the remains of the brooding adult

this nesting pattern was used by another small theropod, *Troodon*, which arranged its eggs in concentric circles—a ring within a ring. A nest of *Troodon*—found in Montana and initially misidentified as belonging to the small plant-eating dinosaur *Orodromeus*—consisted of 24 eggs arranged in this manner. Other small, meat-eating dinosaurs probably used a ring strategy similar to that of *Oviraptor* or *Troodon*. The most eggs ever found in a single nest were of this type and arranged in this manner. The nest included 40 eggs that had been layered in tiers. Forty eggs seems excessive, even for a large dinosaur; American paleontologist Gregory Paul suggested that this could imply that some dinosaurs practiced "communal nesting" or nest sharing—a behavior observed in some extant large birds.

The largest eggs found near any dinosaur remains are thought to be from theropods. The eggs are elongate and an extraordinary 21 inches (53.6 centimeters) long. In at least one case, a nest of giant eggs such as these consisted of about 26 specimens grouped in pairs in a large ring about 7 feet (2 meters) across. To which kind of theropod these eggs pertain is currently unknown.

Parental Care

Much of what is known today about dinosaur nests, babies, and parental care began with the pioneering work of American paleontologist John "Jack" Horner (b. 1946) of The Museum of the Rockies in Montana. Together with his students and coworkers from Montana State University, Horner has spent much of the past 25 years studying the stunning remains of eggs, nests, and skeletons found at numerous fossil sites in central Montana. Many of these were associated with the plant-eating ornithopod *Maiasaura*, a large "duck-bill" dinosaur that grew to more than 30 feet (9 m) long. Ornithopods were a major subgroup of ornithischian dinosaurs. Among the findings of Horner's team were hatchlings and baby *Maiasaura*, still in the nest. These hatchlings and babies measured up to 3 feet (1 m) long. Their teeth were well worn and their limb joints were weak. These factors suggested to Horner that the hatchlings were eating but were not capable of leaving the nest to fend for themselves. It became evident to Horner that *Maiasaura* babies remained in the nest for as long as several months, until they could get out on their own. The implications were that the defenseless young dinosaurs needed to be cared for, and that an adult dinosaur had watched over them, protected them from predators, and brought food to the nest for them to eat, like many birds care for their young today.

Evidence for the nesting and parenting habits of theropods is not as extensive as that for ornithopods. Fossils of theropod hatchlings are rarer than those of herbivorous dinosaurs. Intact nests are even scarcer. Because known theropod hatchling specimens appear to have well-developed teeth and limb bones, it might be assumed that they were ready soon after hatching to leave the nest in search for food. At present, however, it is impossible to say whether their parents protected them and taught them how to hunt, or whether the parents abandoned them, as happens with many living amniotes.

The most revealing evidence regarding the parental behavior of theropods is found in several specimens of oviraptorids and troodontids in which adult specimens were found lying on top of clutches of eggs, arms (probably feathered) outstretched. This appears to show brooding behavior in which the adult dinosaur was protecting and warming the eggs with its body to facilitate incubation.

CERATOSAURIA: THE EARLY RADIATION OF THE THEROPODS

The Ceratosauria ("horned lizards") is a group that includes many of the earliest theropods but that also includes several later theropods that retain several primitive features. The earliest ceratosaurs lived during the Late Triassic and Early Jurassic Epochs. Several other prominent lines of ceratosaurs persisted, particularly in regions of the Southern Hemisphere (now South America, India, and Madagascar), well into the Late Cretaceous. The name Ceratosauria is a nod to *Ceratosaurus* (Late Jurassic, Colorado, Utah), a predatory dinosaur with a small horn on its snout, named in 1884 by American paleontologist Othniel Charles Marsh. The clade Ceratosauria was originally created by Marsh to include only *Ceratosaurus*. More than 100 years later, in 1986, Jacques Gauthier retained the name as that of a redefined clade of a much larger number of theropods based on his extensive cladistic analysis.

Ceratosaurs range widely in length, from the swan-sized *Segisaurus* (Early Jurassic, Arizona) to the hulking, 36-foot (11 m) long monster, *Carnotaurus* (Late Cretaceous, Argentina). Although they varied widely in size, ceratosaurs were united by several common anatomical traits that distinguished them from the other major clade of theropods, the Tetanurae. Among their unique skeletal traits were the fusion of several bones of the hind limb (toes, upper

Ceratosaurus confronting *Brachiosaurus*, with *Rhamphorynchus* in the foreground

ankle bones); a modified knee joint; sacral vertebrae that were fused to each other and to the ilia; and the particular shape and flaring of individual pelvic bones. The ceratosaur hand had four fingers, although the fourth was greatly reduced in size—a primitive feature that was lost entirely in later theropods.

Adult skeletons of ceratosaurs also possess visually distinctive structures that may have served as a means of sexual display to attract a mate, or that perhaps came into play as males engaged in head-butting or bumping contests to win a position of dominance in their pack. Several ceratosaurs, including *Dilophosaurus, Ceratosaurus*, and *Carnotaurus*, had distinctive head crests, ridges, or horns; however, because so few individual specimens are known of these taxa, paleontologists at present have no basis on which to determine whether these features represent a sexually dimorphic trait.

Ceratosaurs of the Late Triassic and Early Jurassic

The clade Ceratosauria includes two groups, the Coelophysoidea and the Neoceratosauria. The first of these is made up of theropods from the early radiation of the dinosaurs discussed in *Dawn of the Dinosaur Age*. The group Neoceratosauria includes later theropods that span the Late Jurassic to Late Cretaceous Epoch and that retained some of the primitive features associated with ceratosaurs.

The Coelophysoidea

The Coelophysoidea ("hollow forms") were small to medium-sized carnivores that measured from 3 to 10 feet (1 to 3 m) long with the exception of *Dilophosaurus, Gojirasaurus, Liliensternus*, and *Lophostropheus,* which may have reached 20 feet (6 m). Their skulls were low, long, narrow, and tapered at the tip of the snout. Head ornamentation ranged from small ridges (*Coelophysis*) and crests (*Syntarsus*) to large, double crests (*Dilophosaurus*) that ran along the top of the skull between the nasal area and the brow. As with all dinosaurs, the **maxilla**—the main bone of the upper jaw—had a large opening in front of the orbit. There was a distinctive gap along the upper tooth row where the premaxilla, or front top jawbone, was connected to the maxilla. The body plan of coelophysoids included a long, flexible neck; a lightweight body; and a long, narrow tail. Two excellent examples of coelophysoids from the early radiation of theropods are *Coelophysis* and *Dilophosaurus*, described below.

Coelophysis ("hollow form"). This was a small theropod about the size of a large dog; it is known from Late Triassic formations of New Mexico and Arizona. *Coelophysis* was first described and named by Edward Drinker Cope in 1889, but his material was fragmentary. Not much was understood about this early dinosaur until the discovery of the Ghost Ranch quarry in New Mexico. The paleontologist most closely associated with *Coelophysis* was Edwin Colbert of the American Museum of Natural History.

In the summer of 1947, Colbert was at the end of his fossil-hunting visit to New Mexico. He and his colleagues, after successfully completing the excavation of a phytosaur—a crocodilelike archosaur—were preparing to close up camp and move on to another state to look for more fossils. As field paleontologists often do, they spent their last hours walking about, prospecting for new fossils and making plans for the next field season. Suddenly, one member of the team came running excitedly over a hill. In his hand was the claw of a small dinosaur. Further investigation revealed that more bones were just below the surface where the claw had been found. Colbert decided to stay a few more days and thoroughly evaluate the site. Early during the process he wrote in his field notebook,

> *Continued work in dinosaur quarry. This quarry keeps developing more and more, as we work it. Obviously it is not an isolated skeleton with associated odd bits of bone, but a comparatively extensive deposit containing a number of skeletons.* (*Edwin Colbert,* The Little Dinosaurs of Ghost Ranch)

Colbert himself later said that his entry was "the understatement of the year." His two-week field trip was extended for two months in 1947 and also occupied the summer of 1948. The Colbert team's work resulted in the collection of nearly a thousand specimens from a bone bed that measured roughly 30 by 30 feet (9 by 9 m). From the jumbled and tangled bones found on the Ghost Ranch site emerged

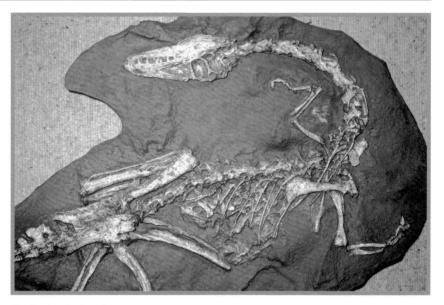

Coelophysis fossil

specimens that ranged in age and size from juveniles to adults and that included several complete, articulated skeletons. It was a once-in-a-lifetime discovery. Colbert's work on this little dinosaur made *Coelophysis* one of the best understood of all dinosaurs.

One of the mysteries of Ghost Ranch was how and why the little dinosaurs met their fate. Colbert reasoned that the animals were traveling together as a group or herd, and all died at the same time, presumably as victims of a mass drowning. They were buried quickly by sand and silt, which prevented scavengers from eating the carcasses. What the herd of *Coelophysis* was doing is still a mystery, and the discovery marks one of the rare cases of finding several individuals of one theropod species in one location. The *Coelophysis* group was clearly larger than a hunting pack. A reasonable explanation is that they may have been migrating or seeking refuge from some natural disaster.

Dilophosaurus ("two-crested lizard"). Known for its peculiar, double-crested head ornamentation, *Dilophosaurus* was a medium-sized theropod measuring 20 feet (6 m) long. It is known from Early

Jurassic deposits of Arizona on the basis of one partial skeleton, two subadult specimens, and several fragmentary skeletons. A crested skull found in China was described as *Dilophosaurus* in 1993, but additional investigation of that material suggests that it may belong to a different, as-yet-unnamed dinosaur. About twice as long as *Coelophysis*, *Dilophosaurus* had a lightweight skeleton that was more similar to its smaller kin than to the bulkier forms normally associated with medium to large theropods. *Dilophosaurus* had the long, lightly built skull of all coelophysoids, but its skull appears taller because of the two parallel head crests that extend along the skull roof from just above the nostrils to just behind the eyes. Seen in profile, the skull of *Dilophosaurus* looks twice as tall as it is because of the crests. There is not enough fossil evidence to speculate as to whether the crest was exclusive to or larger in *Dilophosaurus* males, but if it was, one might surmise that the crest probably made for an impressive display of physical prowess when showing off to a potential mate. The **sacrum**, or fused vertebrae that connect with the pelvis, number only four in *Dilophosaurus*, a primitive feature. Most later and more derived theropods had five or more sacral vertebrae.

Dilophosaurus was relatively lightweight and agile for its length; it weighed perhaps half a ton. This compares with later, more heavily built predatory dinosaurs that may have weighed twice as much at the same length. The forelimbs of *Dilophosaurus* were moderately long, and the three main fingers of its hands were adorned with fairly long, curved claws. The teeth of *Dilophosaurus* varied in size. The longest, most slender, knifelike teeth were in the upper jaw and premaxilla. Among the prey of *Dilophosaurus* were small reptiles and amphibians as well as large, herbivorous "prosauropod" dinosaurs that *Dilophosaurus* probably attacked using a combination of its slashing hand claws and ripping teeth.

The Neoceratosauria

Neoceratosaurs ("new horned lizards") were medium to large predators that measured up to 33 feet (10 m) long. Their skulls were large, tall, and broad, with wide snouts, strong jaws, and large, bladelike teeth. The skull opening behind the orbit was twice or more the size of the orbit. The skulls of neoceratosaurs from the Southern Hemisphere exhibit extensive pitting and sculpting of the bone. Neoceratosaur skulls were adorned with a variety of bony ornaments, including a single stout horn on top of the skull and forward of the eyes (*Ceratosaurus*); a pair of outwardly pointing brow horns over the eyes (*Carnotaurus*); and a bony dome or horn on top of the skull between the eyes (*Majungatholus*). The body plan of a neoceratosaur included a short, stocky neck; long hind limbs; a stout tail; and strong but short forelimbs. The Neoceratosauria lived in the later half of the Age of Dinosaurs and are discussed in more detail in other volumes of *The Prehistoric Earth*.

Living Among the Early Theropods

The early theropods lived among many other kinds of reptilian kin during the Late Triassic. These included larger and more dominant reptilian carnivores that probably kept the early meat-eating dinosaurs in check. The mass-extinction events of the Late Triassic wiped out most of the large herbivores and predators with which the first dinosaurs competed and provided an opportunity for the ruling reptiles to diversify and expand their geographic range.

Joining the theropods in expanding the early horizons of dinosaurs were their saurischian kin, the prosauropodomorphs. These were specialized plant eaters that grew to moderately large size during the Late Triassic and Early Jurassic Epochs. Chapter 5 explores the nature of the sauropodomorphs and their successful radiation into widespread habitats.

SUMMARY

This chapter introduced early theropods and sauropodomorphs that flourished during the Late Triassic and Early Jurassic Epochs.

1. Saurischian dinosaurs are divided into two main groups, the Theropoda (carnivores) and the Sauropodomorpha (large, long-necked herbivores).

2. Theropods are divided into two large groups for discussion: Ceratosauria (Late Triassic to Late Cretaceous Epoch) and Tetanurae (Middle Jurassic to Late Cretaceous Epoch), also including basal Tetanurae.

3. About 40 percent of all known dinosaur taxa of are theropods. All theropods were bipedal predators with strong hind legs and four-clawed toes.

4. There were three basic types of theropod teeth: slender, blade-like serrated teeth; robust, banana-sized serrated teeth; and conical unserrated teeth. The tooth design provides information about the eating habits and attack style of a theropod. A few theropod taxa had no teeth; instead, they had a beak.

5. Theropod feeding styles fall into two general categories based on the design of their teeth and cranial mechanics: "puncture and pull" or "slash and tear."

6. The variation between the males and females of a species is called sexual dimorphism. Visually distinct anatomical features may have been used during courtship for sexual display, to help single out males from females.

7. Early theropods had many kinds of head ornamentation, including nose horns, brow horns, bony skull caps, and head crests.

8. Dinosaurs laid hard-shelled eggs and deposited them in ground-based nests.

9. There is evidence that theropods laid large, elongate eggs and that some small theropods may have sat on top of the eggs in a brooding posture to help incubate the eggs with their body heat.

10. The earliest theropods belong to the clade Ceratosauria, which is divided into two groups, the Coelophysoidea and the Neoceratosauria.

11. *Coelophysis* and *Dilophosaurus* are representative members of the Coelophysoidea.

5

Herbivorous Saurischian Dinosaurs: The Sauropodomorpha

Not all dinosaurs were big. In the case of the sauropodomorphs, however, it is not a question of whether they were big or not, but of *how* big they were. The longest sauropod taxa are sometimes estimated to have been upward of 133 feet (40 m) long. Some may have weighed more than 83 tons (75 metric tons). Thus, compared to the biggest and heaviest land animal known today—the African elephant, at eight tons (7.25 metric tons)—the largest of the sauropod dinosaurs were more than 10 times heavier. Sauropods were second only to whales as the largest vertebrates of any kind ever to evolve.

The tallest, heaviest, and longest animals ever to walk the Earth were members of the saurischian clade collectively known as Sauropodomorpha ("lizard foot form"). In a terrestrial animal, evolutionary adaptations in body size have never been pushed to the anatomical, physiological, and metabolic extremes that were present in the largest of the sauropodomorphs. The first discoveries of their skeletons in the nineteenth century were the catalyst for a craze that continues to this day—a seemingly inexhaustible public appetite for knowledge about dinosaurs. It was the image of the giant, long-necked sauropod *"Brontosaurus"*—now known properly as *Apatosaurus*—that helped skyrocket dinosaurs into the public's consciousness in the 1880s. These most extreme dinosaurs also fueled scientific rivalries across the globe as paleontologists sought recognition for finding the biggest and most complete dinosaur specimens.

The earliest and most basal members of the clade Sauropodomorpha are also known as the "Prosauropoda." "Prosauropods" lived during the Late Triassic and Early Jurassic Epochs. Later, more advanced **Sauropoda** were distributed widely across the globe during the Middle and Late Jurassic Epochs, with some lines continuing in diminished numbers until the end of the age of dinosaurs.

Traits that were shared by all sauropodomorphs included small heads in comparison to the size of their bodies; long necks made up of at least 10 elongate vertebrae; teeth that were adapted for cropping, rather than chewing, vegetation; and small feet with long claws on the first digits of the front feet.

This chapter investigates the traits, lifestyles, and kinds of "prosauropods" and earliest sauropods that lived during the early rise of dinosaurs.

"PROSAUROPODA": THE FIRST HERBIVOROUS DINOSAURS

The "prosauropods" ("before sauropods") make up the smaller part of the sauropodomorph family tree but were clearly successful and geographically widespread in their time. "Prosauropods" represented the first highly specialized adaptive radiation of herbivorous dinosaurs. Their fossils have been found across the globe, including the continents of North America, South America, Europe, Africa, Asia, and Antarctica. Their name refers to their widespread existence prior to the radiation of the sauropods. They gradually disappear from the fossil record during the Early Jurassic Epoch, when sauropods began to supplant them as the dominant herbivores.

Although for many years it was believed that "prosauropods" formed a separate and distinct sister taxon to sauropods, the discovery in 2003 by British paleontologist Adam Yates of a primitive "prosauropod" from Wales helped establish that "prosauropods" were, in fact, members of the Sauropoda. The evolution of various "prosauropods" formed successive steps leading up to the more advanced Sauropoda.

"Prosauropod" Traits and Lifestyle

Prosauropods were medium- to large-sized herbivores that measured from 8 to 33 feet (2.5 to 10 m) long. The "prosauropod" body was stout, with a long neck, a small head, and a long tail. The hind legs of most "prosauropods" were longer and stronger than the forelimbs; this indicates that these animals could walk on two legs at least some of the time.

The teeth of "prosauropods" were small and spatula-shaped, with rough serrations on the marginal edges. This kind of tooth could not be used to chew vegetation once it was in the mouth. Instead, like all sauropodomorphs, the "prosauropods" used their teeth to pluck and strip leaves from branches and swallow them whole. Until recently, it was thought that the job of pulverizing the food was done in the stomach, where stomach stones, or **gastroliths**, mashed the leaves together with digestive juices using strong abdominal muscles. This is a digestive aid known in living birds. Evidence for gastroliths—which were nothing more than small stones swallowed by the dinosaur to help with digestion—has been found within the body cavities of a few "prosauropod" specimens, including *Massospondylus* (Early Jurassic, South Africa) and *Sellosaurus* (Late Triassic, Germany).

Gastroliths are widely accepted as a digestive aid used by several kinds of dinosaurs, but a recent reassessment by paleontologists Oliver Wings and P. Martin Sander of the evidence for use by sauropodomorphs raised serious questions about this assumption. The research of Wings and Sander showed that gastroliths simply are not found in the fossil record of sauropodomorphs frequently enough and in great enough numbers to justify the belief in a birdlike digestive system.

The absence of gastroliths and a birdlike gastric mill in the sauropods naturally raises questions about how sauropodomorphs processed their food. It is generally assumed that sauropods, like all other plant-eating tetrapods, employed some form of bacterial fermentation to break down the nutrients in the vegetation that made up their diet. Fermentation in the gut is generally aided by the ability to pulverize the food into smaller pieces that are easier to digest. Other herbivorous dinosaurs, including the "duck-billed" hadrosaurs, reduced their food to a pulp by chewing it with a impressive battery of broad-crowned grinding teeth. Sauropodomorphs, for the most part, lacked such teeth and therefore must have relied on another mechanism to aid digestion. Without a battery of grinding teeth or gastroliths, it is possible that sauropodomorphs extracted sufficient nutrients from their food by means of a prolonged food-retention time due to their extreme body size, thus providing adequate time to digest food more slowly.

The ability to rise up on its hind limbs probably allowed a "prosauropod" to reach the leaves of higher-growing plants and small trees. The large curved claw on the first digit of the animal's forelimb may have had at least two purposes. The animal could have used the claw to grip an upright plant or tree trunk and thereby steady itself as it reached for food. The claw also would have been a handy defensive weapon to use against the predatory animals, including dinosaurs, that may have stalked the "prosauropods."

The "prosauropod" jaw was designed to improve the efficiency of eating plants, and it had features that evolved separately in other herbivorous dinosaurs and in mammals. Prosauropod teeth were small and were generally of the same size and shape throughout the mouth. The teeth lined the outside of the upper and lower jaws. Because a prosauropod's teeth were used for plucking rather than chewing plants, it was important for the dentition to be aligned in such a way that the upper and lower jaws could work effectively together. Ideally, this would mean that the upper and lower teeth could close tightly on a branch and remove leaves with an economic pull of the head and neck, a movement not unlike that of pulling a rake across the branches of a bush. The structure of the "prosauropod" jaw hinge made this possible. The hinge was positioned low so that when the mouth closed, the teeth of the upper and lower jaws came close together but did not touch. When the mouth was closed, the upper teeth normally overlapped the lower ones. "Prosauropods" probably had roomy cheeks in which to hold plucked food until they swallowed it in bunches. *Plateosaurus* (Late Triassic, Germany) is a typical example of a "prosauropod" with uniformly shaped teeth of the same size. The Chinese basal sauropods *Yimenosaurus* and *Jingshanosaurus,* from Early Jurassic deposits, had longer, more robust upper teeth that overlapped the lower jaw considerably.

There is some debate as to whether "prosauropods" were exclusively herbivorous. Some paleontologists believe that they may also have eaten meat, even if only as scavengers. The line of reasoning for this comes from studies of the small, lightweight nature of the "prosauropods'" skulls and their relatively weakly rooted teeth, which could do no more than pluck vegetation. In some ways, the teeth of "prosauropods" were ideal neither for eating meat nor for eating plants, and the cranial features of the animals' skulls were less well adapted for eating tough vegetation than were the skulls of some of their contemporaries, such as the rhynchosaurs and mammal-like reptiles. And yet other lines of dinosaurs, including the sauropods and ornithischians, were more clearly successful plant eaters and shared some of the jaw features of the "prosauropods," including spatulate teeth. The current consensus is that "prosauropods" were herbivores, but British paleontologist Paul Barrett makes a convincing case that they may have been opportunistic omnivores like the iguana, willing to scavenge carrion and eat small prey.

Prosauropods of the Late Triassic and Early Jurassic

The fossil record of "prosauropods" or basal sauropodomorphs still contains many gaps. Some early "prosauropods," such as *Thecodontosaurus* (Late Triassic, England and Wales), were relatively small animals that measured about 6.5 feet (2 m) long and were probably bipedal. Another group were the plateosaurs, named after *Plateosaurus* (Late Triassic, Europe). *Plateosaurus* measured from 10 to 20 feet (3 to 6 m) long and is one of the best known "prosauropods." Cladistic analysis by British paleontologists Peter Galton and Paul Upchurch identifies as many as six or more enigmatic branches of the "prosauropod" family tree that probably will not be sufficiently resolved without additional fossil discoveries in the field. Descriptions of key members of the "prosauropods" follow.

Thecodontosaurus (Late Triassic, England and Wales). This lightweight "prosauropod" was close to the root of the sauropodomorph line and shows many primitive features. It has many of the features of more derived "prosauropods," yet it is quite small—only 6.5 feet (2 m) long. It had a long, thin tail and a shorter neck relative to the rest of its body. It had a small skull with evenly spaced, leaf-shaped teeth lining the jaws, and the front tip of the dentary was slightly downturned. *Thecodontosaurus* is known from adult and juvenile specimens. Its name means "socket-toothed lizard"; it was given this name because its teeth resemble those of extant lizards but are fitted into sockets like mammal teeth.

Plateosaurus (Late Triassic, Germany). *Plateosaurus* is probably the most studied Late Triassic dinosaur due to an abundance of partial and complete specimens. There are more than 100 specimens of *Plateosaurus*, ranging from a single tooth to complete skeletons, and including 10 informative skulls. Known from more than 40 fossil sites in Germany and central Europe, *Plateosaurus* represents the most familiar form of mid- to large-sized "prosauropod." It was first described in 1837 by German paleontologist Hermann von Meyer, who named it *Plateosaurus,* or "broad lizard," based on the large hind limbs that were part of the fragmentary first specimen.

The jaw joint of *Plateosaurus* was below the line where the teeth of the upper and lower jaw met, a specialization that improved the animal's ability to rake branches with its overlapping teeth to remove leaves. *Plateosaurus* had enormous nostrils that were slightly tipped toward the dorsal surface of the skull. This configuration preceded the later migration of the nostrils from the snout to the top of the skull that continued independently in the sauropods and allowed them to take in larger quantities of food without interfering with their breathing.

Plateosaurus was between 10 and 20 feet (3 and 6 m) long; this made it one of the larger "prosauropods." It probably walked on four legs most of the time but could rise up on its hind legs to pick at tall plants. This gave it an advantage over shorter herbivores that could not reach such vegetation.

Riojasaurus (Late Triassic, Argentina). *Riojasaurus* represented the upper end of the "prosauropod" size range. It measured between 20 and 34 feet (6 to 10 m). *Riojasaurus* was named by José Bonaparte in 1969, after La Rioja Province in Argentina. It is currently known from 20 partial skeletons and one skull found in the foothills of the Andes Mountains in northwestern Patagonia. *Riojasaurus* was in most ways a typical "prosauropod," but it had several unique features. Its teeth were not spatulate, or leaf-shaped, but conical. Its front legs were larger in proportion to its hind limbs, suggesting that it was more quadrupedal than most other "prosauropods," perhaps because of its larger girth.

Anchisaurus (Early Jurassic, Connecticut). One of the first dinosaurs discovered was *Anchisaurus* ("near lizard"), whose bones were found in a rock quarry in Connecticut in 1818. Dinosaurs were barely understood at the time; the bones were at first thought to be human, then reptilian. The fossil specimen was not considered dinosaurian until 1885, when Othniel Charles Marsh recognized the bones to be from a "prosauropod" and gave them the name *Anchisaurus*. Known from a nearly complete skull and skeleton, *Anchisaurus* was one of the small "prosauropods"; it measured only about 7 to 10 feet (2 to 3 m) long. It probably walked bipedally much of the time. *Anchisaurus* was a good example of the typical "prosauropod" body plan: a tiny head; a long, thin neck; sturdy hind legs; robust, clawed hands and feet; and a long torso counterbalanced by the tail. Its jaw joint was below the line of the top tooth row, which permitted the teeth of the upper and lower jaw to overlap in a scissorlike fashion to snip leaves, a characteristic feature of most "prosauropods." A distinguishing feature of *Anchisaurus* was that the first toe on the foot was shorter than the second, the reverse of other "prosauropods."

Massospondylus

Massospondylus (Early Jurassic, South Africa, Lesotho, and Zimbabwe). *Massospondylus* ("elongate vertebrae") is another well-known "prosauropod." Measuring 13 to 17 feet (4 to 5 m) long, this moderately large dinosaur typified the body plan of latter "prosauropods" in the Southern Hemisphere. Found in Africa, *Massospondylus* was much like the European *Plateosaurus*, with the exception of a somewhat lighter skeleton and some primitive features retained in the jaws. The jaw joint of *Massospondylus* was not quite as low as that seen in other "prosauropods"; this made its bite less well adapted for stripping vegetation from branches. Its teeth were coarsely spatulate and similar to those of other "prosauropods." A clutch of fossilized *Massospondylus* eggs recovered in South Africa reveals the tiny skeletons of nearly hatched embryos. The individual embryos measured about 6 inches (15 cm) long. Their legs were about equal in length, and they had no teeth. These two factors suggest that *Massospondylus* hatchlings began life as quadrupedal animals and may not have been able to gather food for themselves.

SAUROPODA: GIANT QUADRUPEDAL HERBIVORES

The largest of the dinosaurs were the long-necked, quadrupedal herbivores of the clade known as Sauropoda. Othniel Charles Marsh, whose own fossil excavations in the American West unearthed many of the most famous of the sauropods, dubbed the group Sauropoda in 1878 after their so-called "lizard feet." Marsh pictured the sauropods as walking on the flats of their padded feet, much like extant reptiles. Marsh was the first scientist to create a life illustration of the sauropod body, which he pictured as having padded feet with splayed toes like a lizard. This view of the feet of sauropods led to the impression that they were slow-moving heavyweights that may have needed to spend much of their time in the water to suspend their enormous girth. Current research favors a radically different view of the sauropods as lighter weight (though still heavy), fully terrestrial giants that, like other dinosaurs, walked, with their tails outstretched, primarily on their enormous toes and not on the pads of their feet.

This book, *Dawn of the Dinosaur Age*, explores the evolutionary roots of the sauropods in the Late Triassic and Early Jurassic Epochs. Most of the sauropods described below are considered basal members of the clade: those taxa that exhibit anatomical trends that were passed along to later, more derived sauropods. The sauropods of the Late Triassic were similar to "prosauropods," but the sauropods of the Early Jurassic had begun to exhibit anatomical changes that improved their mobility and allowed them to grow larger.

The largest and most familiar sauropods—such as *Apatosaurus*, *Diplodocus*, *Brachiosaurus*, and *Argentinosaurus*—lived during the second half of the Mesozoic Era, a time span beyond the scope of this book.

Early Sauropod Traits

The sauropods were the more advanced members of the Sauropodomorpha and shared a common ancestor with the "prosauropods." The "prosauropods" maintained a basic body plan that grew to no more than about 35 feet (10.5 m) in the largest species. They had a jaw joint that was lower than the tooth line of the upper jaw, had three sacral vertebrae, and had longer hind limbs that permitted them to move about on two legs with relative ease. It was on these basal traits that sauropods evolved adaptations that eventually led to their ability to grow to enormous size and to process food to feed their presumably huge appetites.

Anatomical traits of the sauropods that made them diagnostically different from the "prosauropods" and other dinosaurs include the following adaptations.

Quadrupedal posture with complementary changes to limb structure. American paleontologists Paul Sereno and Jeffrey Wilson published an extensive comparative analysis of the anatomical traits of sauropods in 1998. Noting that nearly all saurischian dinosaurs prior to sauropods—theropods and "prosauropods" alike—were largely bipedal animals, they focused their definition of the sauropods on those features that enabled them to function as full-time quadrupeds. The proportions, bone shapes, flexibility, and joint structures found in the legs of sauropods are significantly different from those of "prosauropods" and theropods. One telltale sign of a sauropod is that the femur (the upper hind limb bone) is straight and longer than the tibia (the lower hind limb bone); this was one of the many limb adaptations that enabled the bearing of great weight yet allowed the animals to move about with relative ease.

Four or more sacral vertebrae. Having three sacral vertebrae—the fused backbones connected to the pelvis that provided strength—as is the case in the "prosauropods," is considered an ancestral trait of the sauropodomorphs. Sauropods have four or more sacral vertebrae.

(continues on page 116)

THINK ABOUT IT

The Race to Discover the Giants

Two of the most famous paleontologists in post–Civil War America were Edward Drinker Cope of Philadelphia and Othniel Charles Marsh of New Haven, Connecticut. Both men studied dinosaurs found in the American West in the 1870s and 1880s. After several active years of exploring for fossils in person, both Cope and Marsh found even greater success by hiring crews of fossil hunters to find and dig the bones for them. Though friends as young men, the two became bitter rivals, and their dislike of each other lasted their whole adult lives. Cope and Marsh were fierce competitors in the discovery and naming of new dinosaurs.

In 1877, a schoolteacher named Arthur Lakes wrote to Marsh about some large fossil bones that he had found near the town of Morrison, Colorado. Marsh was curious, but instead of jumping at the chance, he politely offered to identify the bones if Lakes would send them to Connecticut. No deal was struck.

Before long, Lakes discovered more bones, including what looked like a gigantic leg. He wrote to Marsh again. Lakes estimated the total length of the animal at 60 to 70 feet, a figure that must have sounded unbelievably big at the time. This time, Lakes took more direct action. He packed up 10 crates of the bones and shipped them to Marsh at Yale in New Haven, thereby hoping to ignite the scientist's curiosity and loosen his wallet.

As a fallback, Lakes also sent a few of the spectacular bones to Cope in Philadelphia, and Cope was the first to act. Delighted at his good fortune, Cope was unaware that Marsh already had been offered the same fossils. Cope set to work to write a scientific description of the dinosaur, but the dinosaur was not his for long.

Marsh became aware of Lake's advances to Cope and immediately took action to gain the upper hand. Marsh sent Lakes a check for 100 dollars. He also warned Lakes that he wanted the entire specimen, including the bones that Lakes had sent to Cope. Unfortunately for Cope, he had not yet paid Lakes for any of the bones, so he had to pack them up and send them to Marsh in Connecticut.

Edward Drinker Cope

So it was that Othniel C. Marsh identified his first new dinosaur without having set one foot out of New Haven, Connecticut. It was a long-necked sauropod, the first of many such giants to be discovered in the Late Jurassic-age deposits of the western United States. Marsh named

(continues)

(continued)

the animal *Titanosaurus* ("Titan lizard"); it later came to be called *Atlanto-saurus*. Marsh did not have evidence of the animal's long neck. Even so, he declared that this was the largest of "any land animal hitherto discovered." He thought that the complete dinosaur would measure about 50 to 60 feet long from its nose to the tip of its tail.

Cope's disappointment over the Lakes dinosaur did not last long. About 80 miles south of the Lakes location, near Cañon City, Colorado, a school superintendent named O.W. Lucas discovered another fossil bed filled with extremely large dinosaur bones. These fossils dated from about the same time as those from Marsh's quarry, but they were in better condition and easier to dig out. Fortunately for Cope, Lucas contacted him first. Cope immediately bought the first sample bones sent to him by Lucas and hired a crew to help dig the bountiful site. By late summer 1877, Cope had turned the tables on Marsh. He announced the discovery of *Camarasaurus*, another giant, "which exceeds in proportions any other land animal hitherto described, including the one found by Professor Arthur Lakes." Cope also found the neck of *Camarasaurus*, making it one of the best known of the early sauropod discoveries in North America.

(continued from page 113)

This condition began to appear in some of the basal sauropods discussed below.

Enlarged claw and weight-bearing feet. The first digit—the inside "toe"—of each sauropod foot is fitted with an enlarged claw or ungual. There is a marked reduction in the size of the unguals from the inside to the outside toes. The feet and ankles are compact, yet sturdily built as weight-bearing structures.

Shift in the position of the nostrils to higher up on the skull. There was a gradual shift in the position of nostrils from the front of the snout, as in "prosauropods" and theropods, to a place higher up on the top of the skull. In later sauropods, such as the brachiosaurids and diplodocids, the nostrils had migrated well up on the skull and were placed either in front of or even between the eyes on top of the skull. The reason for this changing position in the nostrils is thought to be related to eating. With the nostrils out of the way of the oral cavity, it became easier for sauropods to eat uninterruptedly, without having to pause for a breath. This was a highly efficient adaptation for such huge animals that probably needed to maximize their feeding time each day.

Changes to the jaws and teeth. In "prosauropods," the rows of teeth joined at a fairly sharp angle at the front of the mouth. In sauropods, the front of the mouth was broader and more rounded. The sauropod jaw hinge, located higher than that in "prosauropods," allowed the teeth of the upper and lower jaws to rub together, providing a gripping bite. Although sauropods' teeth were also designed for plucking and not grinding plants, the flexibility of their jaws and the coordinated contact of their teeth improved their ability to consume vegetation. The teeth of sauropods eventually varied among taxa, from broad and spatulate in some specimens to more peglike in others. All sauropods had four premaxillary teeth.

Increased pneumaticity of the vertebral column. During the course of their evolution, the sauropods developed remarkable pneumaticity—the presence of concavities and spaces—in their backbones. This lessened their weight without sacrificing strength. This tendency was especially pronounced in the neck and back vertebrae. Adaptations that lead in the direction of improved pneumaticity of the vertebral column were evident in some of the basal sauropods.

Elongation of the neck. The gradual elongation of the neck is one of the hallmarks of sauropod evolution. With longer necks, these giants increased the reach of their heads to the sides in some species and to greater heights in others, presumably to improve the efficiency of gathering food.

Many of the above traits of the most familiar sauropods began to appear in their earliest ancestors. A gradual increase in the body size was clearly under way by the Early Jurassic. Even the smallest of the early sauropods, such as *Blikanasaurus* and *Vulcanodon*, were about the same length as the mid-sized "prosauropods" at 20 to 22 feet (6 to 6.5 m). The Early Jurassic sauropod *Gongxianosaurus* hinted at the future sauropod tendency toward gigantism by nearing a length of 50 feet (15 m). As quadrupeds, the early sauropods were probably somewhat stockier than most "prosauropods." The bulkier body design and eating tools of the sauropods may have given them a competitive edge when food resources were scarce, such as in times of drought, especially if both kinds of dinosaurs were eating plants of the same variety and of similar heights, which was probably the case. If such a plant-eating contest took place during the Early Jurassic, sauropods must have been the heavyweights, utilizing their effective jaw design to strip leaves from plants and fill their bulky bodies with great ease.

Sauropods of the Late Triassic and Early Jurassic

Fossil evidence for the earliest sauropods is often incomplete and fragmentary. Listed here are some of the best known taxa. Their geographic range was widespread, like that of the "prosauropods." Evidence for basal sauropods has been found on the continents of Africa, Asia, Europe, and possibly North America, South America, and Australia.

Antetonitrus (Late Triassic, South Africa). One of the earliest known sauropods is *Antetonitrus,* from Late Triassic rocks dating from 220 million to 215 million years ago. It lived in what is now South Africa, an area also known for an abundance of "prosauropods." Measuring between 26 and 33 feet (8 and 10 m) long, *Antetonitrus* typified a transitional form between a "prosauropod" and a sauropod. It retained some of the features found in "prosauropods," such as a grasping claw on its front feet and legs and feet that had not yet been optimized like the weight-bearing limbs of later sauropods. Yet the size and bulk of *Antetonitrus* testify to its lifestyle as a quadruped and make it the first known member of the sauropods. The dinosaur is known from a single specimen, probably that of a juvenile, consisting primarily of limb, foot, and vertebral elements. The skull is not yet known. *Antetonitrus* was identified and named by British paleontologist Adam Yates and South African paleontologist James Kitching. Its name means "before the thunder," a poetic tribute to a precursor of the Earth-shaking giants to follow.

Blikanasaurus (Late Triassic, Lesotho). This South African minigiant had the bulk and quadrupedal posture of a sauropod packed into a small frame that measured about 20 feet (6 m) long. Dated to about 216 million years ago, it was slightly younger than *Antetonitrus*. *Blikanasaurus* was named after Blikana Mountain in South Africa and is known from only a few bones of the left hind limb, including the tibia, fibula, and foot bones. These limb elements originally were believed to be part of a heavily built "prosauropod," but paleontologists Paul Upchurch and Peter Galton used cladistic analysis to determine that the limb elements of *Blikanasaurus* more closely matched those of sauropods.

Gongxianosaurus (Early Jurassic, China). This enigmatic and tantalizing specimen was found in China and first described in 1998 by the Chinese paleontology team of Xinlu He, Changsheng Wang, Shangzhong Lui, Fengyun Zhou, Tuqiang Lui, Kaiji Cai and Bing Dai. The only specimen of *Gongxianosaurus* ("Gongxian lizard") lacks most of the skull but has a fairly complete **postcranial** skeleton. This early sauropod dates from the Early Jurassic Epoch. The animal was about 47 feet (14 m) long. Its forelimbs were long, and its femur was straight and longer than the tibia, a trait of the sturdylimbed sauropods. The skull is known only from its premaxilla and some teeth. *Gongxianosaurus* is one of the most complete specimens of an early sauropod.

Kotasaurus (Early Jurassic, India). The Indian sauropod *Kotasaurus* ("Kota lizard") is known from the combined disarticulated—unconnected—vertebrae and leg bones of up to 12 individual specimens collected since 1988, when the creature was first named by Indian paleontologist P. Yadagiri on the basis on a single pelvic bone. The largest known individual of *Kotasaurus* was about 30 feet (9 m) long. Only two teeth have been found. They are leaf-shaped, with smooth edges, and they are more like the teeth of later sauropods than the teeth of "prosauropods." Other affinities with the sauropods include *Kotasaurus*'s great size, its four sacral vertebrae, its pelvic girdle, and its straight femur. *Kotasaurus* also retained some basal sauropodomorph features, including a bump on the upper side of the femur and a node on the ankle bone that is not found in more derived sauropods.

Vulcanodon (Early Jurassic, Zimbabwe). First described in 1972 by Rhodesian paleontologist Michael Raath, *Vulcanodon* ("volcano tooth") was the earliest known sauropod until recent discoveries from the Late Triassic, including *Antetonitrus* and *Blikanasaurus*. Its name refers to the fossil bed where the original specimen was found, which was sandwiched between two lava beds. The animal is known from a partial skeleton and a scapula found separately. At 22 feet (6.5 m) long, *Vulcanodon* was of moderate length. It had spatulate, "prosauropod"-like teeth but otherwise resembled a sauropod in skeletal structure with its quadrupedal posture, four fused sacral vertebrae, and polelike femur. *Vulcanodon* is of interest to scientists because even though it lived during the Early Jurassic Epoch, it still retained many primitive features also seen in older "prosauropods," such as the shape of its pelvic girdle and the digits of its feet.

Tazoudasaurus (Early Jurassic, Morocco). *Tazoudasaurus* ("Tazouda lizard") was recently named by an international team of paleontologists led by Rollan Allain of France. Found in Morocco, the specimen consists of a partially articulated skeleton with skull material. *Tazoudasaurus* was related to the line of sauropods that produced *Vulcanodon* and that formed the foundation of the Middle Jurassic radiation of sauropods known as the Eusauropoda. The jaw of *Tazoudasaurus* had several primitive features. These included a high tooth count in its lower jaw (20 leaf-shaped teeth in the lower jaw); V-shaped, rather than U-shaped, tooth rows; and teeth that did not rub together when the jaw was closed. *Tazoudasaurus* was about 30 feet (9 m) long.

IN THE SHADOWS OF THE SAURISCHIANS

The early saurischian dinosaurs, including the predatory theropods and the herbivorous sauropodomorphs, were clearly the most dominant of the early dinosaurs. Together, they represent the most common dinosaur fossils found in deposits that date from the Late Triassic and Early Jurassic Epochs.

Saurischians were one of the two major clades of dinosaurs. Living in the shadows of the saurischians, and with equally ancient family roots, were the first representatives of the other great dinosaur clade, the ornithischians. This is the clade that included all remaining families of dinosaurs—an extraordinarily diverse group of plated, armored, horned, domed, crested, and otherwise adorned herbivores that blossomed in the Early and Middle Jurassic Epochs and persisted to the end of the Mesozoic, the last days of the dinosaurs.

Chapter 6 describes the early history of ornithischians during the Late Triassic and Early Jurassic Epochs.

SUMMARY

This chapter examined the traits, lifestyles, and members of the "prosauropods" and earliest sauropods that lived during the early rise of the dinosaurs.

1. The clade Sauropodomorpha includes basal members also called "prosauropods" and later, advanced sauropods, all having evolved from a common ancestor.
2. Traits shared by all sauropodomorphs included small heads in comparison to the size of their bodies, long necks made up of at least 10 elongate vertebrae, teeth that were adapted for cropping rather than chewing vegetation, and small feet with long claws on the first digits of the front feet.
3. Prosauropods represent the first highly specialized adaptive radiation of herbivorous dinosaurs. They were medium- to large-sized herbivores that measured from 8 to 33 feet (2.5 to 10 m) long. Their bodies were stout, with a long neck, a small head, and a long tail. Most "prosauropods" could walk on two legs at least some of the time.
4. *Thecodontosaurus* (Late Triassic, England and Wales) was one of the earliest "prosauropods."

5. The largest of the dinosaurs were the long-necked, quadrupedal herbivorous Sauropoda. Anatomical adaptations of the sauropods led to their abilities to grow to enormous size and to process large quantities of vegetation. Sauropods had four sturdy, upright limbs; four or more sacral vertebrae; enlarged claws and weight-bearing feet; long necks; nostrils positioned high on the skull; increased pneumaticity of the vertebral column; and leaf- or peg-shaped teeth for plucking leaves.

6. The early sauropods had a combination of primitive traits inherited from their sauropodomorphs ancestors and derived traits that they passed on to later sauropods.

7. *Antetonitrus* (Late Triassic, South Africa) is the earliest known sauropod.

6

EARLY ORNITHISCHIAN DINOSAURS

Ornithischian dinosaurs make up one of the two major clades of dinosaurs. The ornithischians are united by a generalized design of the pelvis known as a "bird," or ornithischian, hip. The great British paleontologist Harry Govier Seeley originated the clade names of Ornithischia and Saurischia in 1888, during the early days of dinosaur discovery and classification. Of the Ornithischia, Seeley remarked that "In this order the ventral border of the pubic bone is divided, so that one limb is directed backward parallel to the ischium as among birds, and the other limb is directed forward." This is indeed the general shape of the ornithischian dinosaur hip, but it should be noted that birds did not evolve from ornithischians. The origin of birds can be traced to the theropods, the predatory members of the Saurischia.

Fossils of ornithischians are rare until the Middle Jurassic. Their earliest representatives lived among the first saurischians during the Late Triassic but only make the scarcest of appearances in the fossil record. The earliest ornithischians were clearly overshadowed by larger and more numerous saurischian meat eaters and plant eaters. Somehow, however, the small, herbivorous ornithischians persisted. They survived into the Jurassic Period and became the seeds of many great lines of innovative and successful plant-eating dinosaurs. The secret of their success may have been in their teeth and jaws. Ornithischians adapted complex batteries of teeth that allowed them to snip and chew tough plant material. Their method of eating contrasted sharply with that of the sauropodomorphs, whose teeth could pluck but not chew. The innovative jaws and teeth that could chew food allowed ornithischians to occupy an unfilled niche in their habitat where sauropods did not go, eating lower-growing plants and vegetation or parts of plants that needed to be well chewed in the mouth to be of nutritional value.

American paleontologist Kevin Padian has pointed out that ornithischian and saurischian dinosaurs certainly were not unique in becoming a successful early confederation of plant-eating tetrapods. These two groups were preceded by other reptile forms from the Permian and Triassic Periods, especially the hippo-sized pareiasaurs and the two-tusked dicynodonts. The ornithischians, however, began with a simple, triangular, plant-cutting crested tooth and improved the design many times over during the Mesozoic. Eventually, some groups of ornithischians developed some of the most complex and highly specialized plant-eating machinery ever seen.

This chapter explores the traits of Ornithischia and introduces the earliest members of the clade. These earliest ornithischians lived during the Late Triassic and Early Jurassic Epochs.

ORNITHISCHIA: TRAITS AND DIVERSITY

The clade Ornithischia is defined by several anatomical traits shared by all its members. The clade is considered a natural group of dinosaurs sharing a common ancestor. All ornithischians were herbivorous; some were bipedal and others quadrupedal. They ranged widely in size, from small bipeds such as *Heterodontosaurus* (Early Jurassic, Africa) and *Hypsilophodon* (Early Cretaceous, United States, England, and Portugal) that were no more than 3 or 4 feet (1 m) long to the tank-sized horned dinosaurs such as *Triceratops* (Late Cretaceous, western North America) and bipedal "duck-bill" dinosaurs such as *Edmontosaurus* (Late Cretaceous, western North America) that may have been more than 40 feet (12 m) long and weighed more than 3 tons (2.7 metric tons). The ornithischians' diversity grew until, by the Cretaceous Period, they were the most common group of plant-eating dinosaurs—quite a feat for a clade that barely held its own during the rapid rise of the Saurischia.

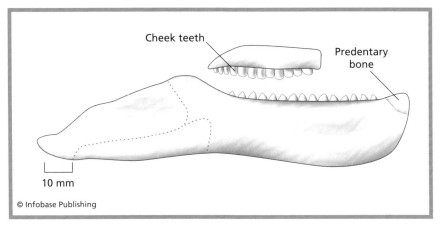

Partial jaw of *Pisanosaurus*

Despite the seemingly vast differences in body size and anatomy of the ornithischians, they are joined by several key traits.

Ornithischian pelvis. The basis for the name of this clade was the presence of a pelvic girdle with a backward-pointing pubis bone.

Predentary bone. Found in all ornithischians, the predentary was a single, scoop-shaped bone that capped the front of the bottom jaw.

Toothless beak. The front tip of the snout (upper jaw) was a toothless beak with a roughened texture.

Leaf-shaped cheek teeth. All ornithischians had leaf-shaped teeth with a triangular crown and narrow roots. Tooth rows were set back from the front of the mouth, in the cheek region. Some later ornithischians developed highly complex batteries of these teeth, specialized for grinding tough plants.

Reduced antorbital fenestrae. The hole, or window, in the skull in front of the eye was reduced in size in the ornithischians.

Eyelid bone. The so-called eyelid or palpebral bone was a narrow bone across the outside of the eye socket, or orbit.

Five or more sacral vertebrae. The number of fused sacral vertebrae added to the strength of the ornithischian frame and aided the animals' mobility.

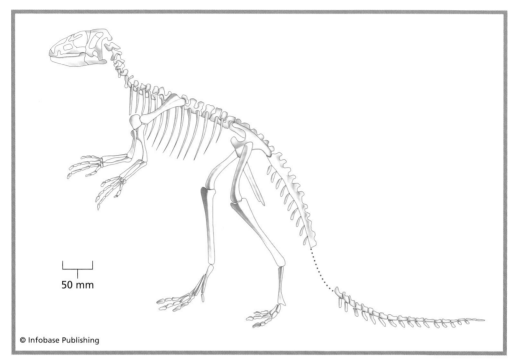

Heterodontosaurus

Reduced fifth toe. The fifth toe of the ornithischian was reduced to a small stub with no joints.

Ossified tendons. Ossified tendons (tendons that turned into bone) located around the sacral region of the vertebral column and, often, the tail provided stiffening for balance.

This list represents the traits that were found in all ornithischians. This set of features also defines a common point of departure from which evolution took off to deliver some of the most unusual, specialized, and ornamented tetrapods ever to walk the planet.

Ornithischia: Clades and Relationships

The basal Ornithischia described below include the best-known examples from the fossil record of the Late Triassic and Early Jurassic Epochs. The origin of the group extends back about 217 million years. In some habitats, such as Lesotho and South Africa, fragments of early ornithischians are found in the same fossil localities as "prosauropods." What little is known of these early ornithischians shows that they were small, bipedal herbivores that exhibited some of the anatomical traits found in all later ornithischians.

From that simple beginning, ornithischians began to diversify by the Early Jurassic. Evidence for the stages of evolution between the basal members of the group and succeeding lineages are poorly known, however. Major clades of ornithischian dinosaurs and their approximate span of existence are shown in the diagram on the following page.

The most recognizable groups of ornithischian dinosaurs include the following clades and members:

Stegosauria. The plated dinosaurs; members include *Kentrosaurus* (Late Jurassic, Tanzania) and *Stegosaurus* (Late Jurassic, western United States); known for the bony plates on their backs and sizable tail (and sometimes shoulder) spikes.

Ankylosauria. The armored dinosaurs; members include *Ankylosaurus* (Late Jurassic, western United States) and *Euoplocephalus* (Late Cretaceous, western North America); known for their extensive body armor and clublike tails.

Basal Iguanodontia. The iguanodonts; members include *Iguanodon* (Early Cretaceous, England, Germany, Belgium, and Spain) and *Tenontosaurus* (Early Cretaceous, Montana, Texas, and Wyoming); known for prominent thumb spikes or sail backs in some species.

Basal Ornithopoda. Early, primitive forerunners of the more advanced iguanodonts and hadrosaurs; members include *Hypsilophodon* (Early Cretaceous, United States, England, and Portugal).

Hadrosauridae. The duck-billed dinosaurs; members include *Edmontosaurus* (Late Cretaceous, western North America); known for their flat, expanded snouts; unusual head crests; and large size.

Pachycephalosauria. The bone-headed dinosaurs: members include *Pachycephalosaurus* (Late Cretaceous, western United States)

Major Clades of Ornithischian Dinosaurs

	Mesozoic		
	Triassic	Jurassic	Cretaceous
	Middle	Middle	
Basal Ornithischia			
Basal Thyreophora			
Stegosauria			
Ankylosauria			
Basal Ornithopoda			
Basal Iguanodontia			
Hadrosauridae			
Marginocephalia			
Pacycephalosauria			
Basal Ceratopsia			
Ceratopsidae			

© Infobase Publishing

and *Stegoceras* (Late Cretaceous, western North America); bipedal dinosaurs with thick, helmetlike bony caps on the skulls of most taxa.

Basal Ceratopsia. The early horned dinosaurs; members included *Psittacosaurus* (Early Cretaceous, China, Mongolia, and Russia) and *Protoceratops* (Late Cretaceous, Mongolia and China); known for birdlike beaks and small, bony neck frills.

Ceratopsidae. The horned dinosaurs; members include *Triceratops* (Late Cretaceous, western North America) and *Chasmosaurus* (Late Cretaceous, western North America); known for enormous neck frills and a variety of nasal and brow horns.

The above groups include some of the best-known dinosaur taxa. Except for the basal, most primitive, members described below, members of the major groups of ornithischians lived during the second half of the Mesozoic Era, from the Middle Jurassic to the Late Cretaceous Epochs. Those ornithischians are explored in detail in other volumes of *The Prehistoric Earth*.

ORNITHISCHIANS OF THE LATE TRIASSIC AND EARLY JURASSIC

The clade Ornithischia is well established and defined, but its earliest members remain largely a mystery. Some are known only from teeth. The best fossil clues to their anatomy are fragmentary at best. Of about 15 specimens tentatively assigned to this group, paleontologists are most confident in the ornithischian nature of the following three taxa.

Lesothosaurus (Early Jurassic, Lesotho). This dinosaur from Africa is the best understood of the basal ornithischians. Paleontologist Peter Galton first described it in 1978, giving it a name that means "Lesotho lizard." It is perhaps the most primitive of all known ornithischians and is understood from four skulls and associated skeletal material. The skull material includes a nearly complete juvenile skull, described by French paleontologist Fabien Knoll in 2002. The skulls clearly show the cheek dentition, made up of leaf-shaped teeth; a small, bony beak on the upper jaw; a predentary; and the characteristic eyelid bone, in this case jutting backward and over the top of the eye socket. *Lesothosaurus* was small, about 3 feet (0.9 m) long, with long legs and a lightly built body. British paleontologist Michael Benton pointed out that the tooth wear seen in the jaw of *Lesothosaurus* suggests that it used an up-and-down chopping motion but had not yet adapted the back-and-forth and sideways jaw mobility that characterizes true chewing motion as seen in later ornithischians.

Pisanosaurus (Late Triassic, Argentina). *Pisanosaurus* was a small herbivore, possibly measuring only 3 feet (0.9 m) long. It is the oldest known plant-eating dinosaur and was nearly contemporaneous with the "prosauropods" of South Africa and South America. The fossil material for *Pisanosaurus* is fragmentary and difficult to diagnose.

Lethososaurus

It was once thought to be an ornithopod (a later line of ornithischi-ans) by paleontologists who studied it between 1967 and 1986, but cladistic analysis by American paleontologists David Weishampel and Paul Sereno in the early 1990s found it to be the most basal of all known ornithischians. Parts of the upper and lower jaw provide the best clues to its affinity, but doubts persist because other por-tions of the specimen are poorly preserved and incomplete. Traits that would unambiguously place it among the basal ornithischians, such as the sacral vertebrae, better pelvic material, and limbs, are missing from this curious and puzzling early dinosaur.

Technosaurus (Late Triassic, Texas). *Technosaurus* was described in 1984 by Indian paleontologist Sankar Chatterjee, who has spent much of his career working with fossil material from Texas. It is known only from a partial dentary—the lower jaw. It was named after Texas Tech University in Lubbock, Texas, where Chatterjee teaches. The teeth are leaf-shaped and positioned in the cheek region. The teeth are closely packed, forming a rudimentary dental battery, a feature also seen in *Lesothosaurus*.

SUMMARY

This chapter explored the traits of Ornithischia and introduced the earliest members of the clade. These earliest ornithischians lived during the Late Triassic and Early Jurassic Epochs.

1. Ornithischian dinosaurs made up one of the two major clades of dinosaurs; the ornithischians are united by a generalized design of the pelvis known as a "bird," or ornithischian, hip.

2. Fossils of ornithischians are rare until the Middle Jurassic. The clade's earliest representatives lived among the first saurischians during the Late Triassic but make only the scarcest of appearances in the fossil record.

3. Ornithischians evolved some of the most complex and effective jaws and teeth for consuming plant material ever seen.

4. The basal ornithischians, although poorly understood, led to several successful lines of later dinosaurs, including plated, armored, crested, bone-headed, and horned herbivores.

5. Ornithischian traits include a pelvis with a backward pointing pubis bone; a predentary bone in the lower jaw; a toothless beak; leaf-shaped cheek teeth; reduced antorbital fenestrae; an eyelid bone; five or more sacral vertebrae; a reduced fifth toe; and ossified tendons along the sacral and tail areas of the vertebral column.

6. The best known basal ornithischian is *Lesothosaurus* (Early Jurassic, Lesotho).

CONCLUSION

The rise of the first dinosaurs is a story of opportunity and evolutionary innovation. The first dinosaurs, after having lived in the shadows of larger reptilian kin, took advantage of major mass-extinction events at the end of the Triassic Period to move into niches once occupied by their predecessors. In the course of doing so, dinosaurs quickly radiated to widespread geographic ranges and began an evolutionary course that led to the development of two major clades of dinosaurs, the Saurischia and Ornithischia.

The Late Triassic and Early Jurassic Epochs were times of experimentation in dinosaur evolution, as the earliest herbivorous and predatory dinosaurs adapted and evolved increasingly specialized body forms and lifestyles. Among the saurischians, carnivorous dinosaurs—having begun as small, lightweight bipedal creatures such as *Eoraptor*—perfected a body plan that provided mobility and quickness coupled with a variety of weapons such as bladelike teeth and recurved claws on their hands and feet. This same body plan would be repeated for millions of years in the continued evolution of predatory dinosaurs, large and small.

The saurischian herbivore body plan—that of a long neck, a bulky body, and a mouth lined with plucking teeth—took shape in the evolution of the "prosauropods" and early sauropods. These dinosaurs rapidly became the largest, most common herbivores of the Early Jurassic and led to the continued perfection of anatomical features suited for supporting great bulk, height, and the ability to consume plant material at enormously productive rates.

The first ornithischian dinosaurs maintained a low profile during the Late Triassic and Early Jurassic, quietly adapting dentition

Tyrannosaurus rex charging

and jaw designs that led to the highly complex, chewing batteries of their descendants. The diversity of later ornithischians is all the more surprising when one considers the simple origins of this clade. The few known basal ornithischians were small, bipedal animals and the first dinosaurs to develop cheek teeth. By the Middle

Jurassic, the ornithischians had spawned the first plated dinosaurs and were soon followed by the parallel evolution of the armored dinosaurs. By the Late Cretaceous, the diverse ornithischians also included enormous bipedal "duck-bill" dinosaurs, bone-headed dinosaurs, and a wide assortment of horned dinosaurs.

Dawn of the Dinosaur Age has dwelt on the foundations of the major clades of dinosaurs, their traits, their adaptations, and their lifestyles. Such were the roots of the dinosaur family tree and the natural events that led to the dinosaurs' rapid dominance of terrestrial life during the rest of the Mesozoic Era.

Appendix One:
Geologic Time Scale

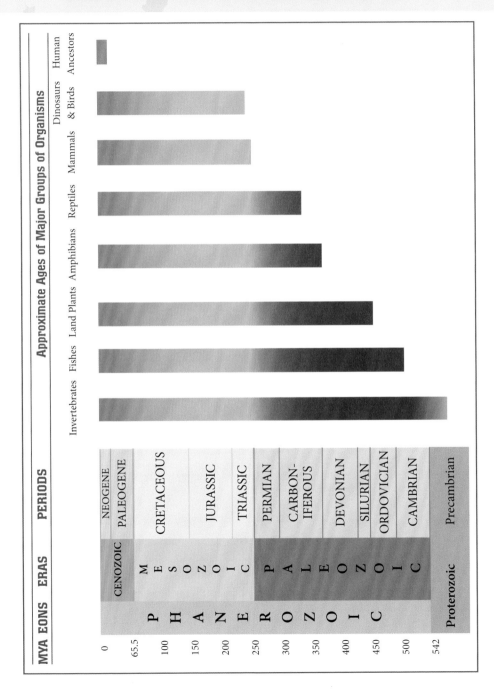

APPENDIX TWO:
ANATOMICAL DIRECTIONS

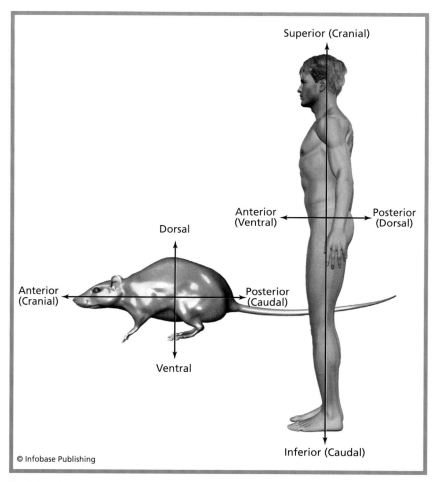

Superior (Cranial)

Anterior
(Ventral)

Posterior
(Dorsal)

Dorsal

Anterior
(Cranial)

Posterior
(Caudal)

Ventral

Inferior (Caudal)

© Infobase Publishing

Positional terms used to describe vertebrate anatomy

GLOSSARY

acetabulum   In a vertebrate, a socket in the pelvic girdle to which the leg bones are connected.

adaptations   Anatomical, physiological, and behavioral changes that occur in an organism that enable it to survive environmental changes.

Anapsida   Amniotes with no temporal fenestrae, including the earliest reptiles.

anatomy   Term used to describe the basic biological systems of an animal, such as the skeletal and muscular systems.

anterior   Directional term meaning the head end of a vertebrate; also known as the cranial end.

antorbital fenestra   In the archosaurian skull, an additional opening in the side of the skull positioned just in front of the orbit, or eye opening.

Archosauria   (archosaurs) The branch of diapsid reptiles that includes dinosaurs, pterosaurs, crocodiles, birds, and their kin.

articulated   Condition of a fossil skeleton found with its bones in place, connected as they would have been in life.

basal   At the base or earliest level of evolutionary development; a term usually used to refer to an ancestral taxon.

bone bed   Fossil locality with a high concentration of bones from more than one individual.

carnivorous   Meat-eating.

caudal   Directional term indicating the tail end of a vertebrate; also known as the posterior end.

clade   A group of related organisms including all the descendants of a single common ancestor.

cladistic analysis   An analytical technique for comparing the genetic, morphological, and behavioral traits of taxa.

climate   The kind of weather that occurs at a particular place over time.

clutch   Group of eggs in a nest.

cranial   The head end of a vertebrate; also known as the anterior end.

cranial process   A forward-pointing extension of the pubis bone.

derived   Term used to describe a trait of an organism that is a departure from the most primitive, or basal form.

Diapsida   (diapsids) Amniotes with two temporal fenestrae: a lower one like the one seen in synapsids and an upper one just above the lower one and behind the orbit.

Dinosauriformes   A clade of ornithodirans more closely related to dinosaurs than to pterosaurs.

era   A span of geologic time ranking below the eon; the Archean Eon is divided into four eras dating from more than 4 billion years ago to 2.5 billion years ago; the Proterozoic Eon is divided into three Eras dating from 2.5 billion years ago to about 542 million years ago; the Phanerozoic Eon is divided into three eras, the Paleozoic, the Mesozoic, and the Cenozoic; the Paleozoic ("ancient life") Era lasted from 542 million to 251 million years ago; the Mesozoic ("middle life") Era lasted from 251 million to 65.5 million years ago; the Cenozoic ("recent life") Era began 65.5 million years ago and continues to the present.

Euryapsida   (euryapsids) Amniotes with one temporal fenestra positioned just above and behind the orbit.

evolution   The natural process by which species gradually change over time, controlled by changes to the genetic code—the DNA—of organisms and whether or not those changes enable an organism to survive in a given environment.

extant   Term used to describe an organism that is living today; not extinct.

extinction   The irreversible elimination of an entire species of organism because it cannot adapt effectively to changes in its environment.

fauna   Animals found in a given ecosystem.

femur   Upper leg bone.

flora   Plants found in a given ecosystem.

forelimbs   The two front legs of a vertebrate.

fossil   Any physical trace of prehistoric life.

gastroliths   Stones swallowed by an animal, often to aid in the crushing and processing of food once it has been swallowed.

gene   A portion of a DNA strand that controls a particular inherited trait.

genus   (plural: genera) A taxonomic name for one or more closely related organisms that is divided into species; names of organisms, such as *Tyrannosaurus rex*, are composed of two parts, the genus name (first) and the species name (second).

gigantism   Unusually large inherited growth traits for a taxon made possible through natural selection.

herbivore   An animal whose primary food source is vegetation.

heterodont   Having different kinds of teeth in different zones of the jaw.

hind limbs   The two rear legs of a vertebrate.

humerus   Upper bone of the forelimb of a vertebrate.

ilium   (plural: ilia) The uppermost bone of the pelvis that is connected to the backbone.

ischium   In a vertebrate, hip bone located below the acetabulum.

Lepidosauria   (lepidosaurs) A group of diapsid reptiles that includes lizards, snakes, and two species of *Sphenodon*—the lizardlike tuatara of New Zealand—and their extinct kin.

mass extinction   An extinction event that kills off more than 25 percent of all species in a million years or less.

maxilla   Major tooth-bearing bone of the upper jaw.

monophyletic   A natural clade of animals descended from a common ancestor.

morphological   Pertaining to the body form and structure of an organism.

natural selection   One of Charles Darwin's observations regarding the way evolution works: Given the complex and changing conditions under which life exists, those individuals with the combination of inherited traits best suited to a particular environment will survive and reproduce while others will not.

Ornithischia   One of the two clades of dinosaurs; the term means "bird-hipped."

paleontologist   A scientist who studies prehistoric life, often using fossils.

Pangaea   Earth's major landmass at the end of the Triassic Period; Pangaea later broke apart into the smaller continents that are known today.

Panthalassic Ocean   The ocean that surrounded Pangaea.

paraphyletic   A clade of organisms consisting of a common ancestor but not all the descendants of that ancestor.

period   A span of geologic time ranking below the era; the Phanerozoic Eon is divided into three eras and 11 periods, each covering a span of millions of years; the longest of these periods, including the three in the Mesozoic Era, are further broken down into smaller divisions of time (epochs).

phylogeny   The family tree of a group of related organisms, based on evolutionary history.

physiology   The way in which an animal's parts work together and are adapted to help the organism survive.

population   Members of the same species that live in a particular area.

postcranial   "Past the head"; term generally used to refer to the portion of the vertebrate skeleton other than the head.

posterior   Directional term indicating the tail end of a vertebrate; also known as the caudal end.

predator   An animal that actively seeks and feeds on other live animals.

premaxilla   The forward-most tooth-bearing bone of the upper jaw.

pubis   Hip bone located below the ilium and that forms the lower front portion of the acetabulum.

sacral vertebrae   Vertebrae that are fused to the pelvis.

sacrum   Series of often-fused vertebrae in the hips, between the ilia.

Saurischia   One of the two clades of dinosaurs; the term means "lizard-hipped."

Sauropoda   (sauropods) Clade of large, long-necked, herbivorous dinosaurs.

Sauropodomorpha   Clade of archosaurs including "prosauropod" and sauropod dinosaurs.

sexual dimorphism   Variation between the males and females of a species.

species   In classification, the most basic biological unit of living organisms; members of a species can interbreed and produce fertile offspring.

Synapsida   (synapsids) Amniotes with one temporal fenestra positioned somewhat behind and below the orbit.

taxon   (plural: taxa) In classification, a group of related organisms, such as a clade, genus, or species.

temporal fenestrae   Openings or "windows" in the vertebrate skull, just behind the orbit on the side and/or top of the skull (the temple region).

Tethys Ocean   The ocean that bounded Pangaea on the east.

tetrapods   Vertebrate animals with four legs as well as two-legged and legless vertebrates descended from them; tetrapods include all amphibians, reptiles, mammals, and birds.

Tetrapoda   The clade consisting of the common ancestor of all living tetrapods and all its descendants.

Therapsida   (therapsids) A group of synapsid reptiles that includes the ancestors of the first mammals.

Theropoda   (theropods) Clade of archosaurs that includes all carnivorous dinosaurs.

topography   Geologic character (elevation differences) of the Earth's crust.

transitional   Term used to describe a fossil representing one step in the many stages that exist as a taxon evolves.

CHAPTER BIBLIOGRAPHY

Preface

Wilford, John Noble "When No One Read, Who Started to Write?" *New York Times* (April, 6, 1999). Available online. URL: http://query. nytimes.com/gst/fullpage.html?res=9B01EFD61139F935A35757C0A9 6F958260. Accessed October 22, 2007.

Chapter 1 – The Mesozoic World

Berner, Robert A. "Atmospheric Oxygen Over Phanerozoic Time." *Proceedings of the National Academy of Sciences of the United States of America* 96, no. 20 (September 28, 1999): 10955–10957.

Chumakov, N.M. . "Trends in Global Climate Changes Inferred from Geological Data." *Stratigraphy and Geological Correlation* 12, no. 2 (2004): 7–32.

Ellis, Richard. *No Turning Back: The Life and Death of Animal Species.* New York: HarperCollins, 2004.

Goddéris, Yves, Louis M. François, and Ján Veizer. "The Early Paleozoic Carbon Cycle." *Earth and Planetary Science Letters* no. 190 (2001): 181–196.

Jacobs, David K., and David R. Lindberg. "Oxygen and Evolutionary Patterns in the Sea: Onshore/Offshore Trends and Recent Recruitment of Deep-Sea Faunas." *Proceedings of the National Academy of Sciences of the United States of America* 95 (August, 1998): 9396–9401.

Kious, W. Jacquelyne, and Robert I. Tilling. *This Dynamic Earth: The Story of Plate Tectonics.* Washington: United States Geological Survey, 2001.

Palmer, Douglas. *Atlas of the Prehistoric World.* New York: Discovery Books, 1999.

Pechenik, Jan A. *Biology of the Invertebrates*, 5th ed. New York: McGraw-Hill, 2005.

Plummer, Charles C., David McGeary, and Diane H. Carlson. *Physical Geology.* New York: McGraw-Hill, 2005.

Prothero, Donald R., and Robert H. Dott Jr. *Evolution of the Earth*, 7th ed. New York: McGraw-Hill, 2004.

Raup, David M. *Extinction: Bad Genes or Bad Luck?* New York: W.W. Norton, 1991.

———. *The Nemesis Affair*. New York: W.W. Norton, 1986.

Saltzman, Barry. *Dynamical Paleoclimatology: Generalized Theory of Global Climate Change*. New York: Academic Press, 2002.

Shear, William A. "The Early Development of Terrestrial Ecosystems." *Nature* 351 (May 23, 1991): 283–289.

Sidor, Christian A., F. Robin O'Keefe, Ross Damiani, J. Sébastien Steyer, Roger M.H. Smith, Hans C.E. Larsson, Paul C. Sereno, Oumarou Ide, and Abdoulaye Maga. "Permian Tetrapods from the Sahara Show Climate-Controlled Endemism in Pangaea." *Nature* 434 (April 14, 2005): 886–889.

Chapter 2 – Archosaurs: The Ruling Reptiles

Benton, Michael. *Vertebrate Paleontology*, 3rd ed. Oxford: Blackwell Publishing, 2005.

Charig, Alan. *A New Look at the Dinosaurs*. New York: Facts on File, 1983.

Colbert, Edwin H. *The Great Dinosaur Hunters and Their Discoveries*. New York: Dover Publications, 1984.

Currie, Philip J., and Kevin Padian, eds. *Encyclopedia of Dinosaurs*. New York: Academic Press, 1997.

Ellis, Richard. *No Turning Back: The Life and Death of Animal Species*. New York: HarperCollins, 2004.

Fastovsky, David E., and David B. Weishampel. *The Evolution and Extinction of the Dinosaurs*, 2nd ed. Cambridge: Cambridge University Press, 2005.

Fortey, Richard. *Life: A Natural History of the First Four Billion Years of Life on Earth*. New York: Alfred A. Knopf, 1998.

Gould, Stephen Jay, ed. *The Book of Life*. New York: W.W. Norton, 1993.

Norman, David. *Prehistoric Life: The Rise of the Vertebrates*. New York: Macmillan, 1994.

Palmer, Douglas. *Atlas of the Prehistoric World*. New York: Discovery Books, 1999.

Prothero, Donald R., and Robert H. Dott Jr. *Evolution of the Earth*, 7th ed. New York: McGraw-Hill, 2004.

Weishampel, David B., Peter Dodson, and Halszka Osmólska, eds. *The Dinosauria*, 2nd ed. Berkeley: University of California Press, 2004.

Chapter 3 – Dinosaur Origins

Benton, Michael. *Vertebrate Paleontology*, 3d ed. Oxford: Blackwell
   Publishing, 2005.

Charig, Alan. *A New Look at the Dinosaurs*. New York: Facts on File,
   1983.

Currie, Philip J., and Kevin Padian, eds. *Encyclopedia of Dinosaurs*. New
   York: Academic Press, 1997.

Farlow, James O., and M.K. Brett-Surman, eds. *The Complete Dinosaur*.
   Bloomington: Indiana University Press, 1999.

Fastovsky, David E., and David B. Weishampel. *The Evolution and
   Extinction of the Dinosaurs*, 2nd ed. Cambridge: Cambridge
   University Press, 2005.

Lucas, Spencer G. *Dinosaurs: The Textbook*, 4th ed. New York: McGraw-
   Hill, 2004.

Norman, David. *Prehistoric Life: The Rise of the Vertebrates*. New York:
   Macmillan, 1994.

Weishampel, David B., Peter Dodson, and Halszka Osmólska, eds. *The
   Dinosauria*, 2nd ed. Berkeley: University of California Press, 2004.

Chapter 4 – Predatory Saurischian Dinosaurs: The Theropods

Benton, Michael. *Vertebrate Paleontology*, 3rd ed. Oxford: Blackwell
   Publishing, 2005.

Carpenter, Kenneth, Karl F. Hirsch, and John R. Horner, eds. *Dinosaur
   Eggs and Babies*. Cambridge: Cambridge University Press, 1994.

Carpenter, Kenneth, and Philip J. Currie, eds. *Dinosaur Systematics*.
   Cambridge: Cambridge University Press, 1990.

Carpenter, Kenneth. *Eggs, Nests, and Baby Dinosaurs: A New Look at
   Dinosaur Reproduction*. Bloomington: Indiana University Press,
   1999.

Colbert, Edwin H. *The Great Dinosaur Hunters and Their Discoveries*.
   New York: Dover Publications, 1984.

Colbert, Edwin H., and Michael Morales. *Evolution of the Vertebrates*, 4th
   ed. New York: Wiley-LSS, 1991.

Currie, Philip J., and Kevin Padian, eds. *Encyclopedia of Dinosaurs*. New
   York: Academic Press, 1997.

Farlow, James O., and M.K. Brett-Surman, eds. *The Complete Dinosaur*.
   Bloomington: Indiana University Press, 1999.

Fastovsky, David E., and David B. Weishampel. *The Evolution and Extinction of the Dinosaurs*, 2nd ed. Cambridge: Cambridge University Press, 2005.

Gauthier, Jacques. "Feathered Dinosaurs, Flying Dinosaurs, Crown Dinosaurs, and the Name 'Aves.'" *New Perspectives on the Origin and Early Evolution of Birds.* New Haven: Peabody Museum of Natural History, Yale University (2001): 7–41.

Irmis, Randall B., "First Report of Megapnosaurus (Theropoda: Coelophysoidea) from China." *PaleoBios* 24, no. 3 (December 22, 2004): 11–18.

Lucas, Spencer G. *Dinosaurs: The Textbook*, 4th ed. New York: McGraw-Hill, 2004.

Norman, David. *Prehistoric Life: The Rise of the Vertebrates*. New York: Macmillan, 1994.

Paul, Gregory S. *Predatory Dinosaurs of the World*. New York: Simon & Schuster, 1988.

——, ed. *The Scientific American Book of Dinosaurs*. New York: St. Martin's Press, 2000.

Prothero, Donald R., and Robert H. Dott Jr. *Evolution of the Earth*. New York: McGraw-Hill, 2004.

Raven, Peter H., George B. Johnson, Jonathan B. Losos, and Susan R. Singer. *Biology*, 7th ed. New York: McGraw-Hill, 2005.

Rayfield, E.J. "Aspects of Comparative Cranial Mechanics." *Zoological Journal of the Linnean Society* 144, no. 3 (July 2005): 309.

——. "Cranial Design and Function in a Large Theropod Dinosaur." *Nature* 409 (February 22, 2001): 1033–1037.

Romer, Alfred Sherwood, and Thomas S. Parsons. *The Vertebrate Body, Shorter Version*, 5th ed. Philadelphia: W.B. Saunders, 1978.

Schultz, Cesar Leandro, Claiton Marlon Dos Santos Scherer, and Mario Costa Barberena. "Biostratigraphy of Southern Brazilian Middle-Upper Triassic." *Revista Brasilerira de Geosciencias* 30, no. 3 (September 2000): 495–498.

Smith, Joshua B., David R. Vann, and Peter Dodson. "Dental Morphology and Variation in Theropod Dinosaurs: Implications for the Taxonomic Identification of Isolated Teeth." *The Anatomical Record*, 285A:2 (June 28, 2005): 699–736.

Tamaki Sato, Yen-nien Cheng, Xiao-chun Wu, Darla K. Zelenitsky, Yu-fu Hsiao. "A Pair of Shelled Eggs Inside a Female Dinosaur." *Science* 308, no. 5720 (April 15, 2005): 375.

Weishampel, David B., Peter Dodson, and Halszka Osmólska, eds. *The Dinosauria*, 2nd ed. Berkeley: University of California Press, 2004.

Wilson, J.A., and Sereno, P.C. "Higher-level phylogeny of sauropod dinosaurs." *Journal of Vertebrate Paleontology*, Supplement 14:52A, 1994.

Yates, Adam M. "A New Species of the Primitive Dinosaur *Thecodontosaurus* (Saurischia: Sauropodomorpha) and Its Implications for the Systematics of Early Dinosaurs." *Journal of Systematic Palaeontology* 1 (2003): 1–42.

Chapter 5 – Herbivorous Saurischian Dinosaurs: The Sauropodomorpha

Benton, Michael. *Vertebrate Paleontology*, 3rd ed. Oxford: Blackwell Publishing, 2005.

Charig, Alan. *A New Look at the Dinosaurs.* New York: Facts on File, 1983.

Currie, Philip J., and Kevin Padian, eds. *Encyclopedia of Dinosaurs.* New York: Academic Press, 1997.

Farlow, James O., and M.K. Brett-Surman, eds. *The Complete Dinosaur.* Bloomington: Indiana University Press, 1999.

Fastovsky, David E., and David B. Weishampel. *The Evolution and Extinction of the Dinosaurs*, 2nd ed. Cambridge: Cambridge University Press, 2005.

Lucas, Spencer G. *Dinosaurs: The Textbook*, 4th ed. New York: McGraw-Hill, 2004.

Norman, David. *Prehistoric Life: The Rise of the Vertebrates.* New York: Macmillan, 1994.

Weishampel, David B., Peter Dodson, and Halszka Osmólska, eds. *The Dinosauria*, 2nd ed. Berkeley: University of California Press, 2004.

Wings, Oliver. "A review of gastrolith function with implications for fossil vertebrates and a revised classification." *Acta Palaeontologica Polonica* 52, no. 1: 1–16, 2007.

Wings, Oliver, and Sander, P.M. "No Gastric Mill in Sauropod Dinosaurs: New Evidence from Analysis of Gastrolith Mass and Function in Ostriches." *Proceedings of the Royal Society B: Biological Sciences* 274, (1610): 635–640, 2007.

Chapter 6 – Early Ornithischian Dinosaurs

Benton, Michael. *Vertebrate Paleontology*, 3rd ed. Oxford: Blackwell Publishing, 2005.

Colbert, Edwin H., and Michael Morales. *Evolution of the Vertebrates*, 4th ed. New York: Wiley-LSS, 1991.

Currie, Philip J., and Kevin Padian, eds. *Encyclopedia of Dinosaurs*. New York: Academic Press, 1997.

Farlow, James O., and M.K. Brett-Surman, eds. *The Complete Dinosaur*. Bloomington: Indiana University Press, 1999.

Fastovsky, David E., and David B. Weishampel. *The Evolution and Extinction of the Dinosaurs*, 2nd ed. Cambridge: Cambridge University Press, 2005.

Lucas, Spencer G. *Dinosaurs: The Textbook*, 4th ed. New York: McGraw-Hill, 2004.

Romer, Alfred Sherwood, and Thomas S. Parsons. *The Vertebrate Body, Shorter Version*, 5th ed. Philadelphia: W.B. Saunders, 1978.

Weishampel, David B., Peter Dodson, and Halszka Osmólska, eds. *The Dinosauria*, 2nd ed. Berkeley: University of California Press, 2004.

FURTHER READING

Benton, Michael. *Vertebrate Paleontology*, 3rd ed. Oxford: Blackwell Publishing, 2005.

Carpenter, Kenneth, Karl F. Hirsch, and John R. Horner, eds. *Dinosaur Eggs and Babies*. Cambridge: Cambridge University Press, 1994.

Carpenter, Kenneth, and Philip J. Currie, eds. *Dinosaur Systematics*. Cambridge: Cambridge University Press, 1990.

Carpenter, Kenneth. *Eggs, Nests, and Baby Dinosaurs: A New Look at Dinosaur Reproduction*. Bloomington: Indiana University Press, 1999.

Charig, Alan. *A New Look at the Dinosaurs*. New York: Facts on File, 1983.

Colbert, Edwin H. *The Great Dinosaur Hunters and Their Discoveries*. New York: Dover Publications, 1984.

Colbert, Edwin H., and Michael Morales. *Evolution of the Vertebrates*, 4th ed. New York: Wiley-LSS, 1991.

Currie, Philip J., and Kevin Padian, eds. *Encyclopedia of Dinosaurs*. New York: Academic Press, 1997.

Ellis, Richard. *No Turning Back: The Life and Death of Animal Species*. New York: Harper Collins, 2004.

Farlow, James O., and M.K. Brett-Surman, eds. *The Complete Dinosaur*. Bloomington: Indiana University Press, 1999.

Fastovsky, David E., and David B. Weishampel. *The Evolution and Extinction of the Dinosaurs*, 2nd ed. Cambridge: Cambridge University Press, 2005.

Fortey, Richard. *Life: A Natural History of the First Four Billion Years of Life on Earth*. New York: Alfred A. Knopf, 1998.

Gould, Stephen Jay, ed. *The Book of Life*. New York: W.W. Norton, 1993.

Lambert, David. *Encyclopedia of Prehistory*. New York: Facts on File, 2002.

Lucas, Spencer G. *Dinosaurs: The Textbook*, 4th ed. New York: McGraw-Hill, 2004.

Margulis, Lynn, and Karlene V. Schwartz. *Five Kingdoms: An Illustrated Guide to the Phyla of Life on Earth*, 3rd ed. New York: W.H. Freeman, 1998.

Norman, David. *Prehistoric Life: The Rise of the Vertebrates.* New York: Macmillan, 1994.

Palmer, Douglas. *Atlas of the Prehistoric World.* New York: Discovery Books, 1999.

Paul, Gregory S. *Predatory Dinosaurs of the World.* New York: Simon & Schuster, 1988.

———, ed. *The Scientific American Book of Dinosaurs.* New York: St. Martin's Press, 2000.

Prothero, Donald R., and Robert H. Dott Jr. *Evolution of the Earth.* New York: McGraw-Hill, 2004.

Raven, Peter H., George B. Johnson, Jonathan B. Losos, and Susan R. Singer. *Biology,* 7th ed. New York: McGraw-Hill, 2005.

Weishampel, David B., Peter Dodson, and Halszka Osmólska, eds. *The Dinosauria,* 2nd ed. Berkeley: University of California Press, 2004.

Wilson, J.A., and Sereno, P.C. "Higher-level phylogeny of sauropod dinosaurs." *Journal of Vertebrate Paleontology,* Supplement 14:52A, 1994.

Web Sites

American Museum of Natural History. Vertebrate Evolution

An interactive diagram of vertebrate evolution with links to example fossil specimens in the world-famous collection of this museum.

http://www.amnh.org/exhibitions/permanent/fossilhalls/vertebrate/

Bernard Price Institute For Palaeontological Research, University of the Witwatersrand, Johannesburg. Fossil Picture Gallery

Information is provided for a wide variety of South African vertebrate fossils by the Bernard Price Institute for Palaeontological Research.

http://www.wits.ac.za/geosciences/bpi/fossilpictures.htm

Carnegie Museum of Natural History: Dinosaurs in Their Time

Online resource and view of the newly renovated dinosaur hall of one of America's leading natural history institutions.

http://www.carnegiemnh.org/dinosaurs/index.htm

International Commission on Stratigraphy. International Stratigraphic Chart

Downloadable geologic time scales provided by the International Commission on Stratigraphy.

http://www.stratigraphy.org/cheu.pdf

Maddison, D.R., and K.-S. Schulz. The Tree of Life Web Project

The Tree of Life Web Project is a meticulously designed view of life-forms based on their phylogenetic (evolutionary) connections. It is hosted by the University of Arizona College of Agriculture and Life Sciences and the University of Arizona Library.

http://tolweb.org/tree/phylogeny.html

Paleontology Portal. Vertebrates

A resource exploring early vertebrate life, produced by the University of California Museum of Paleontology, the Paleontological Society, the Society of Vertebrate Paleontology, and the United States Geological Survey.

http://www.paleoportal.org/index.php?globalnav=fossil_gallery &sectionnav=taxon&taxon_id=16

Peripatus. Paleontology Page

A privately compiled but exhaustive resource on many paleontology subjects, including a valuable look at the Burgess Shale fossils.

http://www.peripatus.gen.nz/Paleontology/Index.html

Public Broadcasting Service. Evolution Library: Evidence for Evolution

This resource outlines the extensive evidence in support of both the fact and theory of evolution, basing its approach on studies of the fossil record, molecular sequences, and comparative anatomy.

http://www.pbs.org/wgbh/evolution/library/04/

Royal Tyrrell Museum, Dinosaur Hall

Virtual tour of a dinosaur fossil exhibit housing Canada's foremost collection of dinosaur fossils.

http://www.tyrrellmuseum.com/peek/index2.php?strSection=9

Scotese, Christopher R. Paleomap Project

A valuable source of continental maps showing the positioning of Earth's continents over the course of geologic time.

http://www.scotese.com/

Virtual Fossil Museum. Fossils Across Geological Time and Evolution

A privately funded, image-rich educational resource dedicated to fossils. Contributors include amateur and professional paleontologists.

http://www.fossilmuseum.net/index.htm

PICTURE CREDITS

INDEX

ABOUT THE AUTHOR

THOM HOLMES is a writer specializing in natural history subjects and dinosaurs. He is noted for his expertise on the early history of dinosaur science in America. He was the publications director of *The Dinosaur Society* for five years (1991–1997) and the editor of its newsletter, *Dino Times*, the world's only monthly publication devoted to news about dinosaur discoveries. It was through the Society and his work with the Academy of Natural Sciences in Philadelphia that Thom developed widespread contacts and working relationships with paleontologists and paleo-artists throughout the world.

Thom's published works include *Fossil Feud: The Rivalry of America's First Dinosaur Hunters* (Silver Burdett Press, September 1997); *The Dinosaur Library* (Enslow, *2001–2002*); *Duel of the Dinosaur Hunters* (Pearson Education, *2002*); and *Fossil Feud: The First American Dinosaur Hunters* (Silver Burdett/Julian Messner, 1997). His many honors and awards include the National Science Teachers Association's *Outstanding Science Book of 1998,* VOYA's 1997 Nonfiction Honor List, an Orbis Pictus Honor, and the Chicago Public Library Association's *"Best of the Best"* in science books for young people.

Thom did undergraduate work in geology and studied paleontology through his role as a staff educator with the Academy of Natural Sciences in Philadelphia. He is a regular participant in field exploration, with two recent expeditions to Patagonia in association with Canadian, American, and Argentinian universities.